Teaching the Story

Fiction Writing in Middle School

CAROL BALDWIN

Maupin House Publishing

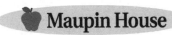
Maupin House

Teaching the Story:
Fiction Writing in Middle School
Carol Baldwin
© 2007 Carol Baldwin
All Rights Reserved

Cover and Book Design: Marble Sharp Studios

Library of Congress Cataloging-in-Publication Data
Baldwin, Carol, 1953-
  Teaching the story : fiction writing in middle school / Carol Baldwin.
      p. cm.
  ISBN-13: 978-0-929895-95-6 (pbk.)
  ISBN-10: 0-929895-95-9 (pbk.)
  1. Language arts (Middle school) 2. English language--Composition and exercises--Study and teaching (Middle school) 3. Creative writing (Middle school) I. Title.
LB1631.B26 2007
808'.0420712--dc22

                    2006033892

Thanks to Joy Acey, Robert Elmer, and Crawford Killian for giving me permission to adapt their work. Thanks to Michelle Flowe and Steve Matchett for granting permission to reproduce their work.
Excerpts from "World Building" from Jeffrey A. Carver's online course, *Writing Science Fiction and Fantasy*. This work was originally published in CD-ROM format by MathSoft, Inc., of Cambridge, Massachusetts. It now appears online at www.writesf.com. Copyright © 2005 by Jeffrey A. Carver. Used with permission.

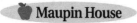

Maupin House Publishing, Inc.
2416 NW 71st Place
Gainesville, FL 32653
1-800-524-0634 / 352-373-5588
352-373-5546 (fax)
www.maupinhouse.com
info@maupinhouse.com

Publishing Professional Resources that Improve Classroom Performance

10 9 8 7 6 5 4 3 2 1

Dedication

This book is dedicated to my parents, Henry and Margaret Federlin, who first believed in me as a writer.

Contents

Acknowledgements

A book isn't written in a vacuum. The community that supported me while I wrote this one included my family, who provided moral and technical support, and the Charlotte, NC Society of Children's Book Writers & Illustrators critique group.

In addition, this book would not have been possible without the tremendous support which I received from the administration and faculty at Carmel Christian School and Covenant Day School. Van Wade, the headmaster at Carmel Christian, and Scott Dillon, the principal at Covenant Day, were willing to let me test the materials in their classrooms. I gathered feedback from many teachers who used this book, but special thanks go to Miriam Franklin, Rita Nichols, Bonnie Williams, Lisa Fogg, Robi Rego, Belinda Johnson, Susan Williams, and Patti Collins who each contributed suggestions. Thank you to Cecelia Tabler who first expressed the idea that "the red pencil is a writer's best friend" and to Maity Schrecengost and Mark Devish who demonstrated that fact to me with my own manuscript.

Thanks to my friend Beth Schulz who prayed with me and for me throughout this project. Special thanks go to fellow writer and teacher, Linda Phillips, who tirelessly walked through the book from inception to conclusion. Finally, I appreciate the students who first tried out these materials and those who allowed me to use their writing samples in this book.

Introduction

Why Teach Creative Writing?

Maybe you don't feel like a writer yourself. Maybe you dismiss creative writing out of habit, thinking you have to focus on assigning "real" writing (like five-paragraph essays on the symbolism in *Romeo and Juliet*). Maybe you've hidden behind the fear that teaching creative writing is an insurmountable mountain better left for next year's teacher to climb.

But maybe you just need a step-by-step unit to take the mystery out of an enigmatic process.

There's no doubt about it—writing short stories is challenging, and teaching your students how to write them may seem out of your range. However, the instructional blocks in this book break down the process of creating a short story into manageable lesson plans that are teacher-friendly and fun. As your students proceed from examining literature to brainstorming the three basic story elements of character, setting, and problem, they will discover story ideas bubbling up from their imaginations faster than they can write them down. You will be amazed at how quickly and easily they embrace the process.

Expository writing is often emphasized in middle school. While that's appropriate—middle-school students are now ready to write essays which explain, instruct, and convince in greater depth than they could do in the elementary grades—the emphasis on the expository can sometimes neglect the middle-school student's blossoming creativity. Your students are reading more intricate novels, they are thinking new thoughts, and they are stretching the wings of their minds and imaginations. Teaching your students the craft of short story writing is a great way of challenging them and channeling their creative energy into a written format. And in the end, teaching your students to write fiction will benefit their expository writing. They will be able to use the skills they develop while writing creatively to add interest, and detail to all their writing.

Your students will be doing more than just brainstorming story ideas. After analyzing the elements of successful stories, your students' hard work begins as they learn how to translate their story ideas into a written piece of work that is readable, entertaining, and perhaps even meaningful. Through many rounds of drafting and rewriting, they will discover how to *show* rather than *tell* a story.

This unit will also help your students prepare for standardized testing, including the new writing section of the SAT. As they move through the process of translating brainstormed thoughts into cohesive writing, they will learn the importance of planning and writing in a logical, sequential manner.

In addition, when students critique their own and their peers' writing, they use critical thinking skills to analyze and evaluate. All these skills are stressed in the National Language Arts Standards developed by the NCTE and IRA (particularly standards 1, 2, 4-6, and 11-12). You can see the full list of standards at http://www.ncte.org/.

All writers work to perfect their craft by constantly searching for the right word or sentence to convey their meaning. Don't be afraid to let your students know how much you are learning also. As you lead your students, I hope this creative process will not only work its excitement in your classroom but also in another writer-to-be—you.

How This Book Is Organized

This book is divided into six blocks of mini-lessons: **Discussing the Basics**, **Creating a Character**, **Setting the Scene**, **Developing the Plot**, **Writing the First Draft**, and **Editing & Revising**. Each block is prefaced with information which provides you with a broad picture of your goals and what your students should achieve in that block of mini-lessons. Each mini-lesson includes instructive material for you to convey to your student as well as classroom activities and homework assignments.

The blocks and mini-lessons are organized in what I think is the most sequential, logical order, and you might decide to use this unit exactly as it is presented. But the mini-lessons are unnumbered so that you may pick and choose just the ones you want to use. The only lesson I recommend not eliminating is **A Look at the Whole Picture** (p. 21), which gives your students an overview of this unit and spells out your expectations for your students. There may be some lessons which you'll decide not to use. For example, if this is your students' first exposure to writing a short story, then some of the mini-lessons (such as **Dialogue** on page 62) might be more than you want to cover.

Blocks and mini-lessons within the blocks can be rearranged. For instance, you might decide to let your students brainstorm a plot before they work on developing a character. Or, you might want to provide a fun introduction to creating stories and begin the unit with the **Three Story Elements** mini-lesson (p. 23). No matter where you start, your students will begin to have ideas about the other story elements. Encourage them to write these ideas down in their binders and return to them when the class begins to work on those lessons.

You will probably re-visit some of the mini-lessons throughout this unit of study. For example, you will refer to **The Red Pencil Is Your Best Friend** (p. 31) many times as your students write their descriptive paragraphs and rough drafts.

Your students will learn how to develop the three main story elements during the **Character**, **Setting**, and **Plot** blocks. Many students will decide to use the characters and settings they brainstorm in the lessons for their stories. Other students might discover that the character or setting they brainstormed doesn't work well with the plot they wanted to use and decide to create a different character or setting. Change happens. Train your students to think about their stories as fluid literary creations that will not be finished until "The End."

Included in the text are the reproducibles and transparency masters your students will need for writing a non-genre-specific story. These worksheets are printed in the book so you can easily reference them as you are working through the different instructional blocks. (The ones that are marked "Transparency Master/Reproducible" are the ones that I recommend discussing in class as well as handing out to all students as worksheets.) They are also included on the Resource CD which accompanies this book, saved in folders named after the chapter in which they appear.

The Resource CD also includes genre-specific versions of many of the reproducibles and transparency masters presented in the book. Use these if your students are writing genre-specific stories or as additional examples of the concepts you are teaching.

In most cases, the files on the Resource CD are saved as Rich Text Format (.rtf) files, so they should be compatible with most word-processing programs. You can customize these to meet your students' needs and re-save the files to your computer for later use. Also, please note that these files are formatted as reproducible worksheets to hand to your students. You may wish to increase the size of the font before printing them to use as transparency masters so they'll be easier to read when on the overhead. (For a complete list of all the reproducibles, see page 138.)

Remember that the transparency masters and reproducibles are only tools to help your students get their imaginations started. They are not traditional "worksheets" that must be filled in line by line (although you should encourage your students to do so). When demonstrating the reproducibles on the overhead, emphasize how they guide a writer into useful, creative discoveries about their stories.

You will also find a teacher/parent letter on the Resource CD (in the Chapter_1 folder) that introduces the unit to your students' parents and solicits their help. If you decide to have a party or writing contest at the end of the unit (see **After "The End"** on page 133), you can also use this letter to request help for these activities. Customize the letter and send it home several weeks prior to beginning this unit.

Instructional Themes

Your instruction will be framed by three themes. While working through the unit, your students might get tired of hearing you say, "How can you *show* that, not *tell* it?," "What are the key details that you want to include?," and "The red pencil is your best friend." However, these three instructional themes are the heart of this unit, and more than likely your young writers will need to hear you repeat them many times as you learn and write together.

Story Showing vs. Story Telling

"Show, don't tell" is a slogan that gets drilled into every writer's mind. Don't *tell me* about the student who doesn't pay attention in school: *Show me* the glazed look in his baby blue eyes when his teacher calls on him, his slouched shoulders, and the *Sports Illustrated* hiding behind his literature book.

Almost all beginning writers (both adult and student) have a tendency to *tell* their stories rather than *show* them through dialogue, action, and the characters' emotions and reactions. This type of narrative distances the writer from the action and leads to boring lists of events such as, "When John went to camp he went swimming, fishing, and hunting. He made new friends and then he came home. The End." This type of writing summarizes the plot. It is *not* the story itself.

Throughout this book you will find many *show, don't tell* examples. Each one shows the difference between descriptive writing that captures a reader's attention and pulls him into a story, and bland, retelling writing. Asking your students to figure out why one type of writing is better than the other will sharpen their critical thinking and show them the importance of incorporating these skills into their own writing.

Show, don't tell is also true for you. You can't merely tell your students about good writing or the importance of revision, you must show them examples. Try out the exercises in this book. Read your results (both good and bad!) to your class. Let them see you develop and grow as a writer. By seeing you struggle to make your character's conflict strong yet simple, or watching you pick the most exact verb, they will realize that writing is a continual process—one in which all writers participate. The **How to Teach This** sections at the end of several mini-lessons are also available on the Resource CD (see the folder named after the chapter that the lesson appears in) so you can easily refer to the examples they provide in your notes when teaching the concepts to your class.

Your students will also be models for one another. As they read their work out loud and the class comments on what makes one piece of writing shine and how another piece could be "jazzed up," they are teaching each other how to become better writers.

Details Make a Difference

One of the main ways that an author shows a character or setting is in the details he chooses. Specific nouns and adjectives—even just a few words—create different types of stories. Consider the difference between stories that include a *soccer* ball, a *base*ball, a *tennis* ball, a *basket*ball, or a *bowling* ball.

Each of these adjectives and nouns immediately conjures up a different image in the reader's mind. Similarly, snow that is *dirty gray* is different from snow that is *ice cream white*, or snow that is *brittle* and *crunchy*. You will have many opportunities to emphasize this concept with your students. Choosing the right details will also help a story be internally consistent. A star quarterback on the junior varsity team who eats half a pizza at lunch and the other half after school probably doesn't take ballet lessons on Friday night and munch on alfalfa sprouts as a bedtime snack.

The Red Pencil Is a Writer's Best Friend

The writing process is never stagnant. Writers constantly delete, change, edit, and rewrite. In fact, many professional writers have a hard time knowing when their work is "done"—the urge to find a better verb, adjective, or simile can prevent a writer from putting her manuscript in the mail. Once a manuscript is accepted for publication, a writer still faces thousands of hours of revision and rewriting. This book, for example, will have been revised dozens of times before it ever reached your hands—and that doesn't include the thousands of changes on the computer which never reached the printed page!

On a smaller scale, this same writing and revising process holds true for your students. Unfortunately, they won't see it exactly the same way.

Typically, students look forward to revising their stories just about as much as they look forward to doing fifty sit-ups or the mile run in PE. They want to finish an assignment, turn it in, and be done with it. They rebel at the thought of revision or correction—their work is perfect, how could it *possibly* be improved? An important part of this unit is showing your students that just like *real* writers, their stories will improve when they take them through several rounds of drafts and revisions. In other words, a red pencil is their best friend— not their dreaded enemy. Their changes and edits, their peers' suggestions and feedback, and your corrections are *part of the entire writing process*—not something that is tacked on at the end before they get a grade.

Whenever you ask your students to find a more dynamic verb, specific noun, or explicit adjective, and when you encourage them to add imagery through similes and metaphors, you are entering into the adventure of cooperative classroom learning. This is guaranteed not to be boring (middle schoolers tend to think more outside the box than adults—their responses will amaze you), and it also pulls students into the creative process. The greater the number of students who contribute to the finished product, the more everyone will feel as if the finished product (a descriptive paragraph, a story from a story prompt, or even just one sentence) is "theirs"—not just the teacher's. As Maity Schrecengost points out in her book *Writing Whizardry*, this "ownership" of the writing piece is essential for students to accept responsibility for changing and revising it.

These important concepts are presented in the **Red Pencil** mini-lesson (p. 31) in the **Discussing the Basics** block but should be reinforced throughout this entire unit.

Teacher Goals

Before you begin, it is important for you to decide what goals you'd like your students to achieve. For example, if you want students to bring their stories to the best level they can, consider allotting additional time for more cycles of critique and revision.

On the other hand, if your goal is for your students to incorporate a brainstormed character into a believable setting, then these reduced expectations will determine not only what you deem to be acceptable work, but how much time you need to allot for students to successfully achieve this goal.

Setting appropriate goals for yourself and your students also will be extremely helpful in determining the parameters of your feedback and conferences. Selecting specific writing skills to focus on will keep you from feeling overwhelmed by the prospect of reading and commenting on a pile of stories. In the same vein, if you anticipate not having a great deal of time to read and make in-depth comments, keep the word limit to between 800 and 1000 words.

Since this unit potentially can be used in consecutive years by members of a language arts team, teachers can benefit from working together to set grade-appropriate goals in conjunction with the language arts goals already established for your school. For example, a student who is writing a short story for the first time will be just beginning to learn how to show rather than tell the story. On the other hand, a student who has already written one should be expected to know that the main character needs to resolve his problem himself and be more proficient at writing dialogue.

Grading, Correcting, and Story Requirements

Your feedback to your students on their descriptive paragraphs, plot sentences, and other written activities should focus on how well they have completed the assignment and on the content of their writing, not on spelling, grammar, and punctuation. A "no grades" policy at this stage promotes creativity and enables students to try out different ideas. Circulate through your classroom while students are completing their in-class assignments. Answer questions and provide assistance.

Deciding how much to have your students edit their "final" story is always a tough call. ("Final" is sometimes difficult for both the student and teacher to decide on since it may be hard to quit working on a story.) Obvious errors in grammar, punctuation, syntax, and spelling must be fixed. These are non-negotiable: to get a satisfactory grade these errors must be corrected. You'll find **Guidelines for Grading Stories**, a suggested grading rubric, on p. 132.

Errors in the story's organization are sometimes more difficult to pinpoint, and may be difficult for your students to fix. For example, you may be able to see that the writer spent far too many words (or pages!) describing unnecessary background information without ever getting to the character's main problem. Or the author may have left out important transitions which showed how a character moved from one event to another. Sometimes too many details stay in the author's mind and never make it to the page so that the story just doesn't make sense. Other times long blocks of description should be interspersed with dialogue. It is important that you point out these major structural observations and suggest appropriate changes.

Whenever possible, the red pencil belongs in your students' hand and not yours. Don't just hand them a marked-up draft: conference with them. Encourage them to take notes. Show them areas they need to consider condensing or reworking.

Remember that although you can see potential changes that might be beneficial to the story, the student must select which changes should be made. Your students' ownership of their stories is vitally important to the writing process. Remember, it is the student's story—not yours.

How to Use This Unit

If you have two weeks or if you have eight, this unit can be adapted to work within your school calendar. First, you can devote several weeks and encourage your students to focus on writing short stories. If you minimize other language arts assignments, your students will respond to this fun activity with enthusiasm.

Second, you could select some of the activities in the **Discussing the Basics** and **Editing and Revising** blocks and integrate them into your school year. For example, you could adapt and use **The Writing-Revising Cycle** (p. 34) or the **Peer Checklist** (p. 129) for other written assignments. In that way, these skills would become an intrinsic part of your students' writing repertoire before they begin this unit.

If you refer to this unit throughout the year, your students will start thinking about their stories ahead of time. For example, as you study the literary devices which authors use, you can remind your class that they can use these elements in their own stories.

Third, you could use this unit during your writing workshops. If you have already allotted at least three blocks of time for writing during the week, this unit is ideal for your classroom. The time to allot for each mini-lesson is indicated at the beginning of each lesson.

Fourth, consider encouraging other teachers in your school to also use this unit. Your middle-school language arts team could decide which genres your school wants to use and when to teach them. In keeping with the types of books which middle-school students seem to enjoy, sixth graders could write a mystery, seventh graders could write science fiction or fantasy, and eighth graders could write historical fiction. One North Carolina school begins this unit in the elementary school where non-genre-specific stories are taught in the fourth grade, sports stories in the fifth, and then the remaining genres in successive grades. Mapping out a plan for your school enables the language arts team to work together and also fends off the, "We did this last year!" complaint from your class—because no, they didn't!

Assigning different genres to different grades also creates a certain amount of "buzz" in your school. You'll hear one student brag about the "awesome sports story" that he is going to write next year or the "unbelievably cool science fiction story" which his best friend wrote last year. The boy who insisted that there was absolutely no way he could write an historical story will surprise you with a vivid description of a Japanese samurai warrior. The girl who absolutely despises science fiction will create an incredible story about robots that transport people into the future. Your students will complain, argue, beg, whine, and nag you to death about switching genres. But in the end, not only will they be writing a wide variety of stories, they will be excited about it, too.

Overview of Blocks

DISCUSSING THE BASICS (CHAPTER 1)

This block of lessons introduces the students to the main instructional themes they will encounter during this unit of study. You will also communicate your goals and expectations for the unit.

CREATING A CHARACTER (CHAPTER 2)

By the time your students have completed this block of mini-lessons, they will be able to brainstorm a character and write a descriptive paragraph that *shows*, not *tells* that character to their reader. They will have practiced creating an information bank and learned how to include key details from that bank in their stories. They will practice building a believable character that is internally consistent. They will focus on creating one or two original characters for their stories that are not shallow stereotypes.

SETTING THE SCENE (CHAPTER 3)

In this block of mini-lessons, your students will go from imagining a setting to *showing* that setting to their readers. They will learn how to brainstorm, select relevant sensory details, and write a descriptive paragraph that creates a mood for their stories. They will focus on creating one or two settings for their stories.

DEVELOPING THE PLOT (CHAPTER 4)

During this block of mini-lessons, your students will define a simple plot for their short stories. By writing a plot sentence, your students will learn to focus on getting their characters (not God, magic, or their best friend) to resolve their own problems. The student writers will outline the events which the character experiences on the way to solving his problem. They will experience the satisfaction of the character reaching his goal or learning how to live with unmet goals or expectations.

WRITING THE FIRST DRAFT (CHAPTER 5)

Equipped with their characters and setting descriptive paragraphs, their plot sentence, and all the reproducibles which they have completed, your students will now be ready to begin their first draft. You will need to remind them that changes they make to any one of the three story elements will affect the other elements—and that is part of the fluid process of writing a short story. They will also need to be reminded not to just dump their information banks or descriptive paragraphs into their stories. Some students may decide to throw out the settings and characters which they had previously brainstormed. This is acceptable, providing they have enough time to create new ones. You will spend less time teaching and more time providing support and direction in short mini-conferences.

EDITING AND REVISING (CHAPTER 6)

After the rough draft is completed, each student's story should be evaluated by himself, a peer, and you. The mini-lessons in this block are geared towards teaching your students to look for their own mistakes as well as to effectively critique one another's work. Ideally, you will be able to read each student's story at least once before they hand in their final draft. Guidelines for grading and strategies for revision are included in this section.

1

Discussing the Basics

Classroom Setup

In order for this creative writing unit to be a success, your students each need their own private workspace in which they can write, undisturbed by their neighbor. Students should have access to classroom copies of a thesaurus and dictionary.

Access to a computer is helpful. The whole process of rewriting and revising is expedited when students can quickly cut and paste electronically. Schedule as much computer time as possible and encourage students to work on their descriptive paragraphs during study halls, etc. To expedite suggestions and corrections, all rough drafts that are to be read by you or peer editors should be typed, double-spaced. Class or homework assignments can be handwritten, but students should skip every other line and write only on one side of the page for ease of reading and receiving feedback.

In this set of mini-lessons, you will give your students an overview of this entire short story unit. You will introduce them to the main story elements, the different types of genres which they can choose from, some crucial revision concepts, and some important tips for writing short stories.

Expectations for Students

All students should bring paper, pens, highlighters, a small package of sticky notes, and a red pen or pencil to every class. They should also bring the book or short story from which they will find good writing examples. (This is discussed further in the **Learn from Literature** section on page 20). They each should have a one-inch binder to keep descriptive paragraphs, the hole-punched reproducibles, and drafts of their stories.

Explain that final stories should be between 800-1600 words (between four to eight typed pages, double-spaced). Students who write stories which are shorter usually have difficulty successfully resolving a character's problem, and students whose stories are longer usually have introduced too many problems or have strayed from the plot idea. Since these are short stories with simple plots, students should focus on creating one or two characters and only one or two settings. If the writer introduces too many plot twists and characters, she will more likely end up *telling* the story, rather than *showing* it.

Emphasize Originality

Middle-school students might not have the no-holds-barred imaginations of three-year-olds, but if they can get beyond what their best friend might think of their stories, they can imagine some pretty creative outside-the-box characters, settings, and plots. Encourage this. Stories that loosely (or not so loosely) resemble TV shows or movies should be discouraged. In the same vein, don't permit take-offs or continuations. You don't want the next Harry Potter or *Lord of the Rings* sequel.

Speaking of three-year-olds, do not allow your students to use animals as their characters. What was appropriate in elementary school is no longer acceptable for middle-school students. Although there are some middle schools novels that use animals in this way (the Redwall series by Brian Jacques or *Animal Farm* by George Orwell) these stories are difficult to write consistently and with authenticity.

Brainstorming Rules

Brainstorming activities are an essential part of this unit. Either as a whole class or in small groups, your students will enjoy the give and take of a brainstorming session. As they bounce their ideas off one another, characters will grow, settings will suddenly materialize, and problems will multiply. Demonstrate the brainstorming process by writing student responses on the board or overhead. Show them how to translate their thoughts and ideas into descriptive writing in group activities.

Your students are going to learn how to brainstorm *information banks* which they will use when writing their stories. Although not all of this brainstormed information will end up in their final stories, these details provide an important depository which the student will draw from when creating richer, more believable stories. Encourage your students to save their ideas in their binders.

As fun as brainstorming can be, it can get out of control. Establish some ground rules. Ideas must make sense, and each additional piece of information must be believable. The Vikings did not discover jungles with poisonous spiders in ancient Rome, a Chinese girl growing up in San Francisco during the early 1900s would probably not be kidnapped by pirates, and twelve-year-old boys rarely tackle armed robbers. Even fantasy and science fiction worlds, as you and your students will discover, must be internally consistent and believable.

If your classroom consists of many verbal individuals who all want to be heard (and what middle-school student doesn't want to express his opinion?), you might want to break the class up into small groups or pairs. Crowd control, as well as your sanity, is as important as the brainstorming process.

Critique Rules

All writers need an audience. Believe it or not, your students will be clamoring to read their descriptive paragraphs and mini-stories aloud in class. This unit includes many opportunities for students to share what they have written in front of the class, with their peer editors, and with you. It is crucial that you establish a fun atmosphere of acceptance and encouragement. Make sure that when your students share their work, all negative critiques are sandwiched in between positive comments. Giving constructive feedback is a vital part of the writing and revising process.

Generate a spirit of cooperation and mutual respect by encouraging your students to listen to one another when they answer questions. As much as possible, encourage them not to interrupt one another. Everyone's feedback is important, but do not allow bossy individuals to dominate the entire class.

In addition, accept input and feedback about your own writing. In doing this you will show your students that constructive criticism is helpful. It also demonstrates that you and your students are a team, working together to make everyone's writing excel.

Story Elements

Every story requires three main elements: *a unique character* that lives in *a particular setting* and has *a pressing problem* which he resolves. An excellent story will also use colorful, descriptive language which *shows* the story to the reader. Your students will learn how to include these criteria in their short stories.

Some students (especially those who are not avid readers and who do not particularly enjoy creative writing) will be satisfied writing a basic, non-genre-specific story that includes each of these story elements. Other students will enjoy the challenge of creating stories that require many genre-specific details.

Genres

In addition to basic instruction in writing a non-genre-specific short story, this unit also provides the opportunity for your students to write a story in any one of four middle-school favorites: sports, mystery, science fiction/fantasy, or history. Since all stories require a character, setting, and plot, the details in these different genres are what make the difference. A lost golden retriever in 21st-century America has a similar plot as a lost unicorn in medieval England—only the characters and setting have changed. A Roman soldier who is angry that he was passed over for a promotion has much in common with a young football player who is angry and hurt when he is not picked to play in the championship game. Many themes, as your students will discover, are universal.

You must decide if your students will all write a non-genre-specific story, the same genre story, or if you will allow each student to pick the genre which he wants to write. The unit is written to be as flexible as possible to meet the needs of your particular class. Some teachers may find it easier for all of their students to work on the same type of story while others may feel comfortable giving their students the opportunity to choose. The mini-lessons are designed to teach the concepts which are necessary to write a short story, no matter what the genre. Examples from the different genres are included throughout the mini-lessons and on the Resource CD. Find out during the genre mini-lesson in the **Discussing the Basics** block how many students plan to write stories in each genre. This will help you tailor your in-class demonstrations.

All students will need a set of the non-genre-specific story reproducibles that you choose. The Resource CD also contains genre-specific versions of many of these same reproducibles. Those students who are writing genre-specific stories (either by their own choice or by your assignment) also will need the reproducibles for the genre in which they are working.

To maximize your students' ability to work independently (and to keep you from having to keep track of all these reproducibles), before you begin this unit you should set up a small hanging file box holder for the non-genre-specific story, and one for each genre that your students will need. If you have access to colored copier paper, print each set of reproducibles on hole-punched paper of a different color. For example, the reproducibles which everyone needs could be printed on white paper and will be stored in the "Story Box." Sports reproducibles could be blue and found in the "Sports Box." Mystery reproducibles could be red and go into the "Mystery Box." Science fiction/fantasy reproducibles could be green, and history reproducibles could be yellow and filed accordingly.

At the beginning of each mini-lesson, write on the board the reproducibles which your class will need that day. As they come into class, students can select what they need and put it into their binders.

Genre Definitions

Here are basic definitions for the different genres that are supported on the Resource CD.

SPORTS

Students should write about a physical activity that is performed as part of a group and involves some type of competition, even if it might not traditionally be thought of as a sport. Playing computer games obviously isn't athletic, but hip-hop dancing, rollerblading, dirt bike or motorcross racing are. Those students who pick non-traditional team sports may need to alter some of the reproducibles to fit their choice. Dancers, for example, have troupes, not teams, and their "playing field" is a studio or auditorium.

You may have a few students who want to write about a sport that is done alone. Rock climbing, for example, is a strenuous physical activity that may include only one other person. Reproducibles can be adjusted for non-team sports.

Obviously, participation in a sport is not a prerequisite for writing this story, but it will enable your students to follow a tried and true writing rule: "Write what you know." Encourage your students to use their knowledge of the sport and relevant details about the game or competition to make their stories authentic.

At the same time, remind them that they are writing *fiction*. You don't want a rehash of Saturday's hockey game with the names changed.

Most students naturally write about a character that is a few years older than themselves. This is preferred over writing about a college student or professional athlete. Most middle-school students don't have firsthand experience about college athletics and therefore will be less likely to write with authenticity.

Your students should create characters who *act*. This is a great opportunity to talk about verb choice. Think about the difference between *walked, ran, jogged, sprinted, sauntered, charged, sped, flew, dashed*, or *darted*. Unless the main character watches a sporting event and becomes inspired to try out, you don't want stories where the main character sits on the sidelines and watches the action. Stories, like sports, are more fun on the playing field than in the stands.

MYSTERY

By definition, anything that is unknown is a mystery. We tend to think that mysteries always involve a crime, but all stories that contain unanswered questions have an element of mystery. A girl whose adoptive parents refuse to tell her about her birth parents, two friends who are baffled by footprints outside their tent, cousins who pry open an old, locked trunk in their grandmother's attic—all these characters face non-criminal mysteries.

Every mystery has several elements in common: a main character acting as the *detective* who wants to find a solution, well-planted *clues* (for the protagonist/ detective as well as for the reader), the antagonist's *motive* to commit the "crime," and *suspense*.

Obstacles serve two purposes in a mystery: they not only prevent the detective from finding the answer too soon, but they also build suspense. The author has reached the story's climax when the reader's suspicions start falling into place— and he *thinks* he knows how the story ends. But remind your students that unexpected twists at the end of the story must be consistent with the clues and lead to a logical resolution.

Given the nature of the mystery story, students need to carefully plan the problem and the clues which their main character finds. A simpler plot (a boy is puzzled by his family's behavior until a surprise birthday party solves the mystery) often leads to a stronger story.

Encourage your students to avoid writing stories which revolve around the FBI, CIA, gangsters, or the Mafia. Since these organizations rarely recruit middle-school students, your classes will not be able to write these stories accurately without relying on clichés from television shows and movies.

Suggest that students think about unusual events which they have wondered about. These "real life" circumstances often trigger good mystery stories. Students should *not* re-write an event which happened to them. Instead, they can use these events as starting points to spin their stories off in a new "what if?" direction.

SCIENCE FICTION AND FANTASY

Science fiction and fantasy writers can construct worlds that have never existed in time, space, or history. Creating societies can feel powerful—remind your students that with power comes responsibility. In these genres, the writer's responsibility is to create a world that *makes sense*. Consistency is crucial—it's acceptable if a character's action defies the laws of gravity as long as the laws of gravity are broken consistently in the story.

In general, science fiction has more new technology and science in it, whereas fantasy can involve mythical creatures and is often based on perceptions of historical cultures. Isaac Asimov said that science fiction, since it is grounded in science, is possible, but that fantasy, which has no basis in reality, is not. Or, as a seventh-grade student once said, neither science fiction nor fantasy is possible in real life, but in the world that's been created, the characters, setting, and problems must be perfectly possible.

There is frequent overlap between the two genres. For example, time travel can exist in either genre but must be consistent within the story. For example, an author writing a medieval fantasy can't include a wizard who transports himself to the future using his laptop computer.

Warn your students that you're going to let them roam into alien worlds and mythical forests. But at some point they'll have to answer the question that every writer must face, "That's great...but does it make sense?"

HISTORY

In order for your students to experience the fun and challenges of writing a story that takes place during a specific historical period, their stories should take place at least thirty years ago. This will also prevent students from arguing that as soon as something happens, it's already a part of history. And no matter how old you are, you will find that to your students, you are already a historical relic!

Encourage your students to do at least a small amount of research in order to make their stories authentic. More than the other genres, historical fiction requires it. Think about the difference between placing a character in a gleaming chariot, a battered covered wagon, or a yellow Volkswagen bus. Immediately, the time period changes. When students ask you if there were horses in Roman times or if there was a drinking age in 1910, your best answer will probably be to direct them to the library or an Internet search engine.

Some students will want to write alternate history stories. A favorite in North Carolina is to have the south win the Civil War. Emphasize that reality must remain consistent in these stories. Jefferson Davis moving into the White House would not cause gravity to fail. The purpose of historical fiction is to present *realistic* events and *believable* characters in a historical setting. Your students' characters should go to school, play with their friends, and argue with their parents just like your students do—except they will do them during a different time in history.

Learn from Literature

Throughout this unit your students will be finding examples of character descriptions, settings, and problems in the books and stories which they are reading. Your students' favorite authors are sharing your task of teaching story composition: they will show your students the end result of many hours of writing and revising—a great story. As the students learn the nuances of writing stories in different genres, they also begin to appreciate an author's hard work in writing an entire novel.

As your students analyze these story components and discover what makes them enjoyable and interesting, they will begin to make the connection between reading and writing. Six words summarize this link: "If you want to write, read!"

You must decide if your students will select their own novel or short story to use as a resource during this unit or if you want everyone to find examples from the same story. If you prefer using short stories as your examples, READ magazine and your language arts anthology are good sources for short stories for your classroom. Also see the **Recommended Reading Lists** on the Resource CD.

Chapter_1: Recommended Reading Lists

Teaching the Story

Mini-lesson

Suggested lesson length: 45 to 60 minutes

A Look at the Whole Picture

Goals

- Provide an overview of this unit.
- Communicate your expectations for what students should accomplish during this unit.
- Assign or allow students to pick a book or short story to be read in conjunction with this unit. (Note: For students who are writing genre stories, it is recommended that the students read a story in the corresponding genre.)
- Introduce *information bank* and *show, don't tell* as concepts.

Teacher Preparation

- Pick a quote from **Advice from the Experts** and write it on the board. Or search the Internet using "writers quotes + writing" and pick your own.
- Put together a variety of objects (books, flowers, toys, etc.) in a convenient place and cover them with a sheet.
- Review the suggestions listed in **After "The End"** (pp. 133) and decide which activities you want to use.

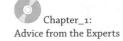
Chapter_1:
Advice from the Experts

Instructional Tasks

Review the entire unit and the time schedule you will follow.

Discuss classroom rules and your expectations as outlined in the preface to the **Discussing the Basics** block of lessons.

Discuss how students will use their self-selected books or short stories as models for good writing.

Explain to your students that throughout this unit they will be brainstorming *information banks* which they will draw from when writing. Explain that although not every detail that a writer brainstorms will go into the final story, these banks will help them create original characters and sensory-rich settings.

Introduce *show, don't tell* as a concept. Ask students to consider which is more memorable: *showing* a pair of boots that your grandpa wore in the rodeo and letting your friends smell the leather, feel how soft it is, and see the bloodstain of the bulls on the sides or *telling* them that "My grandpa has a cool pair of old cowboy boots."

Draw attention to your collection of covered objects. Take the sheet off, wait sixty seconds, and cover them again. Ask students to list what they saw using at least one descriptive adjective for each item. Then direct students to write quick descriptive paragraphs *showing* what they saw.

On an overhead, write a few *telling* sentences that list some of the objects. For example, a sample *telling* sentence could read, "There were a bunch of old books and toys, and one yucky flower arrangement."

Contrast that with some *showing* sentences:

> "Four books were stacked neatly, like a librarian was getting ready to shelve them. The dreary flowers drooped and belonged in an old Victorian bedroom."

If you are going to have a celebration or contest at the end of the unit (see **After "The End"** on page 133), discuss some options with your students. Have them help choose appropriate activities and assign volunteers to different tasks.

Looking Ahead

The **Three Story Elements** mini-lesson uses pictures for story prompts. Invite your students to bring in old family photographs or pictures of someone doing something unusual (or taken in an unfamiliar setting) for the next class.

Mini-lesson

Suggested lesson length: 45 to 60 minutes

The Three Story Elements

Goals

- Help students understand the three main story elements.
- Discuss the fluid nature of story building.
- Lead students through the process of creating a class story.

Teacher Preparation

- Write the following quote on the board:

> "Sometimes you know the story. Sometimes you make it up as you go
> along and have no idea how it will come out. Everything changes as
> it moves. That is what makes the movement which makes the story."
>
> –Ernest Hemingway

- Choose a thought-provoking picture to use as a story prompt and make a
  transparency from it. Ambiguous pictures which can be interpreted in different
  ways, such as those in Chris Van Alsburg's book *Mysteries of Harris*, are fun to
  use. If your students are writing a genre story, use a picture or poster from that
  genre or use the **Genre Story Prompts** (see the Resource CD).

Chapter_1:
Genre Story Prompts

Instructional Tasks

Discuss how the *character* is the "who" in the story—the main person who has
a believable problem which can be solved. Students should limit their stories
to two main characters. Some students will decide that one of these characters
should be an *antagonist*—the person working against the protagonist. Students
will learn to show their characters **FAST**:

Feelings

Actions

Speech

Thoughts

Discuss how the *setting* is the "where" in the story. The more fully the writer
shows the reader what this place looks, feels, sounds, or smells like—the more
real the place will be in the reader's mind. Students should limit themselves to
not more than two settings.

Discuss how the *plot* is the "what happens" in the story. For a story to be more than just a boring list of what happens to a character between the time he gets up in the morning and the time he goes to bed at night, the character must have a goal and a problem reaching that goal. The events in the story should be believable and consistent with the character and setting.

Discuss Hemingway's quote. Explain that stories can begin with any of the three story elements (character, setting, or plot). But as writers create their stories, each of the elements may change as new components add shape to what they have already written. Let them know that writers often have to change and delete sentences, paragraphs, and even pages as their stories develop.

Using one of the picture prompts, brainstorm what could be happening in the story. Encourage students to do more than just say what will happen next. Highlight how "No one saw when Claudia's mother pushed her into the bottom of the boat" is more exciting than "I think that this picture is about a group of Cubans who are trying to escape."

List student sentences on the board and vote on which one to develop. Using class input, write six to eight sentences that begin to tell this story on the overhead. Remind students that the story must use the picture in an appropriate way. At the end of the lesson, highlight the *character*, *setting*, and *plot* in the mini-story that the class has written.

Variations

Put the picture prompt on the overhead and ask each student to write a sentence to begin the story. Encourage students to think beyond obvious possibilities. Each student then passes the sentence to a neighbor who adds another sentence. Circulate the stories around the class until they return to the original author or until ten to fifteen sentences have been written. Read the (often hilarious!) results. This exercise demonstrates how the same visual prompt can elicit different stories.

Divide the class into groups of five students. Using photographs which the students brought in, distribute five different pictures to each group, clipping a piece of notebook paper to each picture. Each student writes one sentence to begin the story and then passes the picture and paper to another student who adds to the previous sentence. Let the stories go around the group twice. Ask the group to pick one of the stories to read out loud to the class.

If you're not using a genre picture prompt, you can put one of the Genre Story Prompts on the overhead. Using the last sentence in the prompt as their launching points, students can generate mini-stories using the same process as described above.

Tip: *Remind students that* storytelling *isn't the same as* story writing.

Tip: *Encourage students to start their stories as close to the problem as possible.*

Mini-lesson

Suggested lesson length: 15 to 20 minutes

Details Make a Difference

Goal

Communicate the importance of writers using specific, key details in their stories.

Teacher Preparation

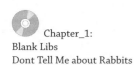

Chapter_1:
Blank Libs
Dont Tell Me about Rabbits

- Choose one or two **Blank Libs** from the Resource CD and make copies. (These **Blank Libs** are fill-in-the-blank stories that the student completes with nouns, verbs, and dialogue.)
- Make copies and a transparency of **Don't Tell Me about Rabbits, Show Me 'de Tails'** (p. 28).

Instructional Tasks

Consider the following examples:

EXAMPLE #1:

Two immigrants arrive lonely and poor in New York City. One is a nine-year-old girl named Ruth Slovotksy, who emigrated from Russia in 1911. The second is a fifteen-year-old girl named Rita McCaulley, who emigrated from Ireland in 1848.

EXAMPLE #2:

Compare these two paragraphs:

"The log cabin looked bright and cheerful after the spring rain. Colorful flowers lined flower beds that were carefully maintained. A soft breeze perfumed the air."

"Spider webs clung to the log cabin's walls. Untended flowers poked forlornly through the weeds. An autumn wind, sounding like a lonely fife, piped among the trees."

Hand out **Blank Libs**. (The first two lend themselves to fantasy and science fiction.) Students may create character names, imaginary objects, and events to

Teaching the Story

fit the context of the mini-story. Whenever possible, students should not repeat a word. After ten minutes, ask volunteers to read their Blank Libs. Point out how inserting different details creates totally different mini-stories.

Looking Ahead

Hand out **"Don't Tell Me about Rabbits, Show Me 'de Tails."** This was one of Ellen Johnston-Hale's (a late North Carolina writer) favorite sayings. (This reproducible is adapted from materials developed by Joy Acey, another North Carolina writer.) Ask students to write out their responses.

"Don't Tell Me about Rabbits, Show Me 'de Tails"

—Ellen Johnston-Hale

Shades of Meaning

1. What is your favorite color? Make a list of words that show that color. (Example: Orange—pumpkin pie, navel orange, scissors handle, fall leaf, tangerine)

2. What is your favorite smell? Make a list of words that show that odor. (Example: Spicy—Pizza cooking, crushed chili peppers, Italian sausage grilling, cinnamon apples baking)

3. What is your favorite taste? Make a list of words that show that taste. (Example: Mint—candy cane, spearmint gum, peppermint ice cream, grandma's tea)

4. What is your favorite texture? Make a list of words that show this texture. (Example: Soft—velvet, rabbit fur, baby's skin, toddler's hair, puppy's belly)

5. What is your favorite sound? Make a list of words that show this sound, using onomatopoeia if you would like. (Example: Drums—crash, boom, rat-a-tat-tat, bong)

Disgusting Descriptions

1. What is the worst color you've ever seen? Make a list of colors you hate or that you'd never be caught wearing. (Example: Liver brown, baby-barf green, cat-puke yellow)

2. What is a smell that makes you pinch your nose? Make a list of smells that turn your stomach. (Example: Bathroom odor, skunk stink, boys locker room, rotten fish)

3. What is a taste that makes your mouth pucker? Make a list of taste words that shut people's mouths. (Example: Sour milk, fried chicken liver, cow's intestines, lemon slices)

4. What is something that doesn't feel good? Make a list of touch words that are strictly hands off. (Example: Hair-sprayed hair, a splinter from a bleacher, oven-hot pavement, sweaty t-shirt, cold bacon grease, slimy oysters)

5. What are some sounds that make you want to cover your ears? Make a list of sound words that will have people racing to find ear plugs. (Example: Dogs yowling, a leaf blower's clatter, police sirens, nails on a chalkboard)

Mini-lesson

Genres

Goal

Provide a brief overview of each genre so that students can decide which genre they want to pick. Although all stories require the same three elements, students who write genre stories will add genre-specific *details* to their characters and settings.

Teacher Preparation

Make transparencies and copies of the four Defining the Genre reproducibles found on the Resource CD. Remember to print different genres on different color paper.

Chapter_1:
Defining Historical Fiction
Defining Mystery
Defining Sci-fi Fantasy
Defining Sports

Instructional Tasks

Review the following genre definitions. Discuss books or stories which students have read and the genre-specific details which the author used.

Point out how a character's problem, such as a broken bone, could be changed to match the genre. Review this example:

NON-GENRE STORY

A thirteen-year-old boy breaks his arm just before completing his project for the regional science fair.

SPORTS STORY

A young golfer breaks his leg before try-outs.

MYSTERY

Who turned off the lights so that the skater fell and tripped and broke her arm?

FANTASY

The prince fell off his unicorn and broke his arm, so he can't joust during the Unicorn Games.

HISTORY

The messenger boy breaks his leg and can't deliver an important message for General George Washington as was planned.

Poll the class and determine how many students plan to write stories in each of the genres. It is also acceptable to write a non-genre-specific story that takes place in ordinary settings in current times.

Briefly review the **Defining the Genre** reproducibles with your students. At this point, your students should use these handouts to help them decide which genre they want to pick. Later, they will fill them out when they are brainstorming their stories.

Looking Ahead

Consider decorating your room with posters, pictures, books, and magazines that illustrate the genres your students will be writing in. Ask them to bring items from home to hang in your classroom.

Mini-lesson

Suggested lesson length: 20 to 30 minutes

The Red Pencil Is Your Best Friend

Goals

- Emphasize the importance of revision throughout the writing process.
- Help students identify their own reluctance to being edited and different points in the writing process when editing should occur.

Teacher Preparation

Make a transparency and copies of **The Writing-Revising Cycle** (p. 34).

 Chapter_1: Writing-Revising Cycle.pdf

Instructional Tasks

Ask students to think about what they dislike about making changes when writing a story or essay.

Point out that revision happens on many levels: ideas generated in the brainstorming process are thrown out, words are crossed out and replaced with better ones, punctuation is changed, phrases are added, sentences are totally deleted because they sound awkward or don't make sense, paragraphs and scenes are re-arranged. Share your own painful "red pencil" stories with your students. (My editing experiences include an editor cutting out 30,000 words from my first book. Similarly, before this book found its way into your classroom, it had been reorganized and rewritten more than five times.)

Instruct your students to line-out, rather than erase, the changes that they make. Encourage them to save the various drafts of their stories, and to occasionally review them. Sometimes writers end up returning to earlier choices. As Nancie Atwell points out in *In the Middle*, students learn about the writing process when they review the stages which they went through to create a finished product.

Using **The Writing-Revising Cycle** transparency, point out that the writing process is circular rather than linear. Each change a writer makes affects not only what he writes next, but may also change what he has written previously.

Using student input, write two boring, wordy sentences on the board (see **How to Teach This**, next page). Ask students to help you line-out dull verbs and tired nouns and replace them with more vivid verbs and specific nouns. This activity can be repeated several times or done in pairs. Hand out copies of **The Writing-Revising Cycle** for students to keep in their binder.

Tip: *You are an important model of this revision process. As your students watch you modify your own writing on the board, they will learn to do the same. The give-and-take process which you generate with your students by leading them into dialogues like, "I don't like my verb/noun/adjective in this sentence. It's too boring and not very specific. How can we jazz up this writing?" shows them how real writers write.*

Chapter_1
How to Teach—Red Pencil

How to Teach This

You can teach this concept by writing a few simple sentences on the board. You can ask for student input in making up sentences on the spot, or you can use the following example.

> "Maryanne walked into the room. She looked around her and was surprised that no one noticed her."

After writing that, I could decide that *walked* is boring, so I could line it out and put in either *sneaked, strutted, skipped, stormed, pranced, cartwheeled*, or any number of other verbs. Then I could specify what type of room Maryanne entered. Was it a grand ballroom? A farm house kitchen? A computer lab in a space modular? Each of these specific details would not only change the setting but would also influence the description of Maryanne's behavior. Now, depending on the changes I made, I would have to see if the second sentence still made sense and what new changes were necessary. The new sentences could read:

> "Maryanne strutted into the locker room. She glared around her and was shocked that no one noticed her."

By substituting *strut* for *walk*, *glare* for *look*, and *shocked* for *surprised*, and by placing Maryanne in the locker room, I have begun to create a much more interesting, visual scene. But then I might decide that *strut* doesn't really fit the anger in the word *glare*.

> "Maryanne stormed into the locker room. She glared around her and was shocked that no one bothered to look up. Not one person noticed her."

In this third revision I chose the verb *storm* which prompted the addition of the *no one bothered to look up* phrase. I then added the final sentence for emphasis, but it doesn't seem strong enough:

Teaching the Story

"Maryanne stormed into the locker room. She glared around her and was shocked that no one bothered to look up. Not one of her supposed friends seemed to notice her."

Substituting *supposed friends* for *person* sets the scene for more conflict and also hooks the reader into wanting to read more.

The writing-revising cycle is invaluable as your students learn that revision is an integral part in creating vivid characters and settings which *show*, rather than *tell*, their stories.

The Writing-Revising Cycle

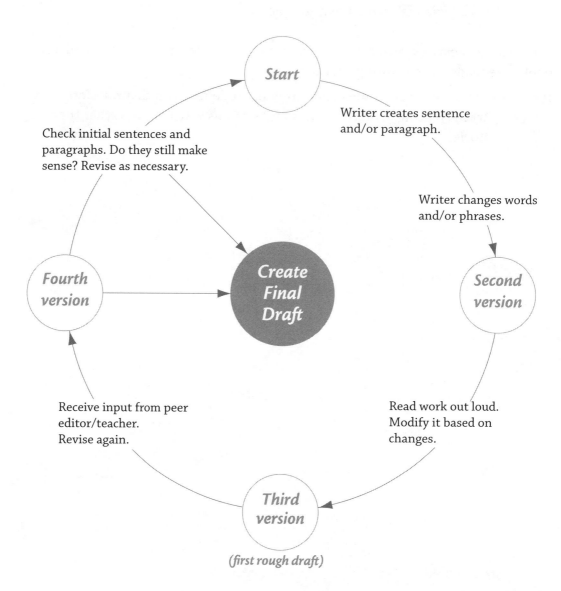

Start

Writer creates sentence and/or paragraph.

Check initial sentences and paragraphs. Do they still make sense? Revise as necessary.

Writer changes words and/or phrases.

Fourth version

Create Final Draft

Second version

Receive input from peer editor/teacher. Revise again.

Read work out loud. Modify it based on changes.

Third version

(first rough draft)

Mini-lesson

Background Research

Goal

To help students use appropriate resources when gathering background information for their stories.

Teacher Preparation

- Check out some *Eyewitness, Facts on File, How Would You Survive, See through History, Metropolis*, or *Inside Story* books from your library. These types of books are great for their details and pictures.

- For more serious reference, you might consider having some of the following available:

  Brooks, Terry. *The Writer's Complete Fantasy Reference*.

  Gerrold, David. *Worlds of Wonder: How to Write Science Fiction and Fantasy*

  Rose, C. *Giants, Monsters & Dragons: An Encyclopedia of Folklore, Legend, and Myth*

  Writer's Guide to Everyday Life, series. This series includes a tremendous amount of details from different time periods.

- Bring in an example of a family artifact. (Examples: A great-great-grandmother's sun bonnet, a wooden stethoscope used in Germany in 1922)

- On the Resource CD is a reproducible called **Helpful Websites for Research**. Add your favorites and save the file to your hard drive. Remember to periodically check to make sure the addresses haven't gone bad. Make copies and laminate them for display near the class computer.

Chapter_1: Helpful Websites for Research

Instructional Tasks

Discuss how writers create authentic characters and settings by researching and selecting key details. Refer back to the **Genres** mini-lesson (p. 29) and use a novel or story which the class has read for examples. For example, the Statue of Liberty was dedicated in 1886. If a student's story is about German-Jewish immigrants coming to the United States in 1870, the Statue of Liberty would not have welcomed them.

On the overhead, list resources that the students can use for background research. Include

- Nonfiction books
- Pictures and maps online or in encyclopedias
- Family pictures, artifacts, and stories
- Historical novels
- **Helpful Websites for Research**

Variation

Provide classroom time for students to go the media center and research their area of interest using books or the Internet.

Tip: *Students only need a few key details to make their stories accurate and believable. Warn them not to get side-tracked as they research!*

Mini-lesson

Suggested lesson length: 15 to 20 minutes

Whose Point Is It Anyway?

Goal

To help students compare the point of view from which stories are told so that they will select one for their stories.

Teacher Preparation

Make a transparency and reproducibles of **Whose Point Is It Anyway?** (p. 38).

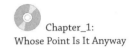

Chapter_1:
Whose Point Is It Anyway

Instructional Tasks

Put **Whose Point Is It Anyway?** on the overhead and discuss the advantages and disadvantages of point of view.

- Compare novels or short stories that are written from different points of view.
- Third-person examples: *A Handful of Time* by Kit Pearson, *The Island* by Gary Paulsen, *Dicey's Song* by Cynthia Voigt.
- First-person examples: *Walk Two Moons* by Sharon Creech, *Journey to America* by Sonia Levitin, *A Walk to Remember*, by Nicholas Sparks.
- Omniscient examples: *Salmandastron* by Brian Jacques, *The Scarlet Letter* by Nathaniel Hawthorne.

Classroom Activity

Using the first-person narrative included on **Whose Point Is It Anyway?**, have students rewrite it in third-person limited, and then in third-person omniscient. Discuss the differences.

Whose Point Is It Anyway?

FIRST PERSON

The narrator relates the events that she witnesses and participates in. Although a first person narrative is very personal and immediate, the author is limited to including only the events which the narrator can see and hear.

THIRD-PERSON LIMITED

The most common point of view; the story is written about "he" or "she." The main character is the focus of the action, and the author reveals everything through this character's feelings, thoughts, or actions. The reader moves through the story along with the main character. Again, the author is limited to only the events which take place in the narrator's presence.

THIRD-PERSON OMNISCIENT

Also written about "he" or "she." However, the narrator doesn't have to stick with only one character. The reader can see events in several settings from several characters' points of view. Third-person omniscient is more complicated to write.

Exercise

Rewrite the following first person narrative in third-person limited, and then in third-person omniscient.

> "I hate my stupid math teacher," I announced, plopping my books down on the kitchen counter. "I just know he has it in for me."
>
> My father looked up from his morning cup of coffee. "What's wrong this time, Jared?" he asked me.
>
> "Look at this grade he gave me!" I shoved my latest math fiasco in front of his newspaper. "I got every answer right. But he took off all these points for all of this other garbage that he said I did wrong. Because of him I ended up with a C⁻! You're on the school board—I don't know why you guys put up with teachers like him!"
>
> I could see my father's face flush as red as his coffee mug. I knew math hadn't been his best subject either, and I was hoping for a little sympathy in that department. Boy, was I wrong.

*Mini-lesson*

Thematically Speaking

Goal

To help students consider a possible theme for their stories.

Teacher Preparation

None.

Instructional Task

Good stories will have a universal theme which resonates with the reader. Pick a story that the class has recently read and discuss the author's theme. How did the author *show* this theme? How was it integrated into the story? Write these themes on the board.

Classroom Activity

Review this list of common themes and ask students if they can add any others.

1. Acceptance of self in spite of feeling or being different
2. Getting over a fear/courage
3. Faith/hope/love prevails
4. Good vs. evil
5. Honesty
6. Loyalty
7. Justice/peacemaking
8. Sacrifice
9. Maturity
10. Perseverance

Ask students to copy this list and circle the theme they might want to use in their stories. Remind them that they will not be locked into any particular theme and that themes may change during the process of brainstorming character, setting, and plot.

Mini-lesson

Suggested lesson length: 15 to 20 minutes

Hints and Reviews

Goal

Provide students with quick guidelines to reference while they're writing their stories and review the key points of this **Discussing the Basics** lesson block.

Teacher Preparation

Chapter_1:
Ten Hints
Tips 4 U

Make a transparency and copies of **Ten Hints for Writing Great Short Stories** (p. 41) and **Tips 4 U** (p. 42)

Instructional Task

Hand out copies of **Ten Hints for Writing Great Short Stories** and **Tips 4 U** and discuss.

Ten Hints for Writing Great Short Stories

1. Use direct, action verbs. "She ran," instead of "She was running."

2. Make sure your verb tenses remain consistent throughout the story.

3. Show, don't tell: "The rose smelled like fine French perfume," instead of "The rose smelled pretty."

4. Paint a picture with words. "Saliva drooled unnoticed down his wrinkled face," instead of "The old man couldn't take care of himself."

5. Use your imagination. What is your character feeling? Why does he make certain choices? What does your character think? What makes him angry, depressed, happy, excited, or confused?

6. Create imagery using metaphors and similes. "Her hair was like wet spaghetti plastered to her face."

7. Each paragraph should only have one main subject. Change paragraphs when a new person speaks.

8. Keep your stories simple. Make sure you are familiar with the time and place where it takes place. The main character should face a conflict and grow as a result of it.

9. Intersperse narrative and dialogue.

10. Don't start with "Once upon a time," and don't end with "They lived happily after." Start with action, not background information.

Tips 4 U

Write what you know—Part I. Your feelings or experiences can be the beginning of a story. You'll be able to write about an event or emotion with greater authenticity if you have experienced it yourself.

Write what you know—Part II. If you write about a place that you have visited, you can write with greater realism. If you haven't been there, research the area so that you can accurately describe it.

Make your character move. Write what your character thinks or feels as he is *doing* something. How does his behavior *show* what he feels or thinks?

Keep it short. In a short story the setting must be a small part of the whole. Don't write long narrative paragraphs describing the setting.

Let your main character do the work. Don't solve the problem too quickly or too easily. Don't rely on magic, God, or a best friend to solve your character's problem.

Keep the characters and settings to a minimum. Don't include more than two main characters and settings.

Keep the problem simple. The more complicated problem you give your character, the more difficult it will be for him to resolve it himself.

Don't moralize. If you are writing a story with a moral, let the character learn it through the events and people in the story.

For contest & publication submissions, follow the guidelines carefully.

- Keep within the word length requirement.
- Include all necessary personal information.
- Double space your manuscript.

Let your imagination go and have fun!

2

Creating a Character

In this block of mini-lessons your students will learn how to brainstorm a believable character.

A logical precursor to developing a fictional character is learning to express thoughts and feelings about oneself. The mini-lesson called **Getting to Know You—The Author** helps students write about themselves as a springboard to writing about their characters' conflicts and emotions. Although this activity is geared towards self-exploration, students can also use it when they are brainstorming their characters.

The *show, don't tell* principle is highlighted in the second mini-lesson through examples from literature, student samples, and in-class activities. Next is learning how to *show, don't tell* by brainstorming a character. In the third mini-lesson your students will have fun creating characters in class and then on their own. Your job, besides crowd control, will be to emphasize that it is important to create internally consistent characters and that key details will *show* those characters to readers.

Three short mini-lessons complete the block. In the first, students will consider the connotations a character's name can carry. The next has students brainstorming an antagonist, and the last is about writing dialogue. Depending on the time you have allotted for this unit and the goals you have set for your class, you may or may not choose to include these mini-lessons.

Although many students will use the characters and antagonists that they develop in this block of mini-lessons for their stories, others may decide to start the process over when they actually begin writing their first drafts. Remind your students that an integral part of the writing-revising cycle is that change happens. Encourage your students to expect it.

Getting to Know You—The Author

Goals

- Help students understand themselves as writers.
- Encourage students to build upon their own experiences to create realistic characters with believable problems.

Teacher Preparation

Chapter_2:
Getting to Know You

Make copies of **Getting to Know You—The Author**. (This inventory of personal likes, dislikes, and history is found on the Resource CD.) Make extras if you want students to fill out a copy for a fictional character.

Instructional Tasks

Introduce the idea that a student's own feelings and experiences can be a good springboard to their stories. For example, a student who remembers how it feels to be embarrassed in front of her peers will be able to show a character in that situation with much greater authenticity. That writer will be able to show a character's hot, red face and how she wishes that the floor would open up and swallow her whole—because she remembers a similar event in her own life. Specific, memorable experiences can trigger impressive stories which impact readers.

This does not mean that students *must* have experienced everything their characters experience. But, it's a good jumping-off place.

Hand out **Getting to Know You—The Author**. After students have completed it, discuss their answers. Ask them to consider if they wrote down any emotions or experiences which they might use in a story.

Looking Ahead

Students can begin brainstorming by filling out another **Getting to Know You—The Author** for a fictional character.

Ask students to use a sticky note to mark a sample paragraph from their reading in which the author *shows* the character to the reader.

Mini-lesson

Suggested lesson length: 45 to 60 minutes

Show, Don't Tell Your Character

Goals

- Demonstrate how authors of students' self-selected novels and short stories show their characters to their readers.

- Encourage students to think about the *show, don't tell* concept through in-class critiquing of student samples.

Teacher Preparation

- Make a banner that reads "If you want to write, read!" and display it in your classroom.

- Using a book which the class has read, create a transparency that vividly *shows* a character. If your class is writing a genre story, pick a paragraph from that genre.

- Make a transparency of **Show, Don't Tell—Create Real Characters** (p. 47). Remember that there are genre-specific versions of this reproducible on the Resource CD. Make sure they are available for your students and incorporate them into your discussion as appropriate.

- Make copies of **Who Is This Character?** (p. 48).

- Write a quote from **Advice from the Experts** (in the Chapter_1 folder on the Resource CD) on the board.

Chapter_2:
Show Dont Tell Character
Who Is This Character

Instructional Tasks

SHOW, DON'T TELL FROM LITERATURE

Ask for volunteers to read their paragraphs from the **Getting to Know You** handout. Comment on sentences which *show* who the person is, rather than just *telling* about him. For example, "I hate math because my father grounds me whenever I get a C on a test, which is all the time," *shows* more about a character than "I hate math because I always get Cs."

Read the character example you selected. If you made an overhead, ask students to identify the words and phrases which *show* the character.

Invite students to read sample descriptive paragraphs from their self-selected novels or short stories. Encourage students to give feedback about which words and phrases best *show* the character—who he is physically as well as what type of person he is.

Choose one of these characters, and create an information bank of his characteristics. Include outer (physical traits) and inner (his personality) qualities. Ask students to list the nouns, verbs, adjectives, and adverbs which the author uses to paint this picture. Discuss how the author is *showing* the character through key details and not *telling* about him in vague, general terms.

SHOW, DON'T TELL PRACTICE

Put **Show, Don't Tell—Create Real Characters** on the overhead. Ask students to decide what is wrong with the *telling* paragraphs and which words or phrases make the *showing* paragraphs better.

Alternatively, cover up the *showing* paragraphs and ask students to rewrite the *telling* paragraphs. After five minutes, uncover the *showing* paragraphs and allow students to compare their answers to the originals.

Point out how details can define a character. Asking your students, "What is the first thing that you notice when you look at your character?" may help students to think about key details. For example, writing "Samuel walks with a limp" is more descriptive than writing "Samuel looks different than other kids." Writing "In spite of Samuel's limp, he still tried out for the baseball team" *shows* Samuel's spunky personality.

Use any of the genre-specific reproducibles from the Resource CD for genre examples.

Looking Ahead

For homework, hand out copies of **Who Is This Character?** (p. 48).

Show, Don't Tell—Create Real Characters

Telling Paragraphs:

- Ted is eleven years old. He has brown hair and blue eyes. He has a younger brother named John who Ted thinks is a brat. Ted's best friend is Jared and they like to go surfing together. Ted hates to brush his teeth. His mouth smells.
- Anne is thirteen and still likes watching *SpongeBob SquarePants*. It is winter.
- Miguel was nervous as he waited for his name to be called for his driving test.
- The man who killed the cockroach was cold and ruthless.

Rewritten as *Showing* Paragraphs:

- The way Ted figured it, he wasted at least 2.3 minutes every morning and at least 2.6 every night—counting the time it took to walk to the bathroom, take the top off the toothpaste, put the stupid stuff on his toothbrush, brush his teeth, recap the tube, and argue with his bratty little brother about who was going to wash the blue blotches from the sink before they dried into ministalagmites. That was 4.9 minutes a day, which Ted rounded up to five. That was 35 minutes a week, 1820 minutes a year, over 30 hours a year—a whole extra day!—that he could be playing video games or surfing with his best friend, Jared, instead of brushing his teeth.

  As a result, Ted's mouth stunk like a garbage can that hadn't been emptied in months.
- Anne entered the front hall of her house and dropped her snow-soaked boots on the floor. She jumped as a gust of cold air slammed the door shut. Anne walked over to the couch and grabbed the remote. Even at thirteen, she still loved *SpongeBob SquarePants*. (Katherine, 6th grade)
- Miguel shifted nervously from one foot to the other and wished there was a bathroom nearby. The line that stretched down the hall and outside the building hardly seemed to move. Would the examiner ever get around to calling his name? Worse yet, once he was in the car, would he forget to come to a complete stop like the last time he took the test?
- Cockroach-man quickly chopped his bug in half and cleaned his blade with his tongue before pressing the bayonet over his heart. (Steve Matchett, *The Gold of Corozal*, unpublished manuscript, 2000)

Who Is This Character?

Directions

Continue the paragraphs that have been started for you. Include information that shows what the person looks like and what he will do next. How do his actions show what type of person he is?

1. Lloyd's lips curled into a sneer as he walked onto the soccer field.

2. Lisa looked at the referee in shocked disbelief. Tamora had obviously pushed her. Why hadn't the ref called a foul?

3. The palms of Paul's hands felt like wet dishcloths. He really wanted to win this election...but what if the class advisor found out what he had done?

4. Heather pushed through the crowd at the locker room door. She would absolutely *die* if her name wasn't on the varsity cheerleading squad list.

Mini-lesson _____

Suggested lesson length: 45 to 60 minutes

Create a Character Information Bank

Goals

- Show students how to brainstorm a character and develop an information bank using graphic organizers.
- Model writing a descriptive paragraph about a character.

Teacher Preparation

- Write the following quote on the board:

    "My theory is to take somebody you like and get him into trouble—
    that's a recipe for a story. The better the character and the worse the
    problem, the better the story—with the caveat that the character
    has to solve the problem by making a tough choice."

    –Bruce Coville

- Make copies and transparencies of **Create a Character—Make an Information Bank** (p. 54) and **Describe Your Character** (p. 55).
- Depending on the genres your students are working in, make transparencies of one or more of the genre-specific versions of these reproducibles from the Resource CD. You might also want to use the following from the Resource CD:

    - **Create Imaginary Characters**
    - **Key Character Details for Genre Stories**

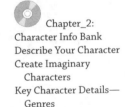

Chapter_2:
Character Info Bank
Describe Your Character
Create Imaginary
Characters
Key Character Details—
Genres

Instructional Tasks

Review that students want to show their characters **FAST**:

Feelings

Actions

Speech

Thoughts

Use **Create a Character—Make an Information Bank** and **Describe Your Character** transparencies to brainstorm a character. Start with a name. Discuss how the name will give clues to the character's ethnic background, parents, and personality and possibly foreshadow the plot. Consider the differences between characters named *Charity, Josephina,* or *Hang Li.*

Write "_____'s Information Bank" on the board and use student input to create the character. All suggestions must be consistent with prior answers. If the class is brainstorming a boy they named Charles Wong whose parents immigrated to the U.S. in 1970 from China, he probably doesn't have bushy red hair.

Make sure that your class doesn't create straight-A, never-gets-in-trouble, perfect characters. Characters, like people, aren't without pimples. If Stephanie is the most popular and prettiest eighth grader, it might be interesting if she was also a cheat or a gossip.

Create some of the character's background by giving him a history. Imagine some of his emotions, motivations, fears, and dreams. Remind students that not all these details will get used in the story, but including them in the information bank will allow them to portray their characters with a natural-feeling depth.

Use **Describe a Character** last. That way, the class is less likely to build a stereotypical, blonde, blue-eyed, buff fourteen-year-old and more likely to create an original personality with out-of-the-ordinary character quirks.

Remind your students that characters should be unique. They should avoid recycling characters from movies, TV shows, video games, or books. Emphasize that the goal is to brainstorm a brand new character.

Discuss creating images by using similes and metaphors. Students can experiment with these figures of speech, making sure that their comparisons make sense and enhance the story. For example, would a rookie soccer player facing his first shootout feel *as scared as a mouse* or *like an actor going on stage the first time*?

If your class is writing a genre story, put **Key Character Details for Genre Stories** on the overhead. Brainstorm some of the key details that a writer should include to make this character come alive to the reader. If your students are writing a genre story, you can use one of the genre-specific **Take It from the Bank** transparencies (see the Chapter_2 folder on the Resource CD) and show how to use an information bank to write a descriptive paragraph.

After ten minutes of brainstorming this information bank, begin writing a descriptive paragraph on the board. As a class, try out different adjectives and similes to see which fit best. For example, when a hockey player is fouled, is his face *as red as a cherry*, *a sunset*, or *a chili pepper*? Ask the class to pick the image which best *shows* the character.

Have students continue writing this paragraph, picking and choosing which details to include without simply listing the brainstormed information. Refer back to the **Show, Don't Tell—Create Real Characters** transparency if necessary.

Students can also use a copy of the **Getting to Know You** handout from the first mini-lesson as an aid to brainstorming their characters.

Ask students to read their paragraphs. If time permits (or as a future assignment), have students use the same information bank to create a character of the opposite gender.

Looking Ahead

For homework, have students use **Create a Character** and **Describe Your Character** to create an information bank about their main characters.

Students should write four to eight sentences that weave together information about this character. Instruct students to focus on one moment in time. What does this person look like right now? What is he doing, thinking, or feeling? This is not the time to write an involved story. Plot ideas should be saved in their binder. Refer them to **Show, Don't Tell—Create Real Characters** for examples.

Ask students to think of other ways their characters might express themselves. For example, what slogan would be on his favorite t-shirt? What type of jewelry does she wear? What is her favorite store in the mall? What kind of music is not allowed in his house? What is her favorite website? Screensaver? How does this character react to his parents' rules? To an enemy's taunts? Write a journal entry or e-mail that this character might write. Answers to these questions provide windows into a character's personality.

Ask students to bring a newspaper or magazine to class for the **You're Going to Name Him What?** mini-lesson (p. 56).

For Stuck Students

If a student is stuck creating a character, suggest that he look at pictures in magazines, the newspaper, or people in any public place: the grocery store, mall, bus stop, library, etc. Encourage students to imagine how the people they observe talk, walk, run, argue with their parents, end a friendship, trash their room, ride a bike, or eat an ice cream cone. Writers learn about their characters when they give them something to do and then imagine how they do it.

Extension

Ask students to write two separate paragraphs showing a character doing the exact same thing with different thoughts, motivations, and emotions. What is the difference between the following two examples?

- Todd shoved his report into the back of his desk. His father would kill him if he saw it!
- Todd carefully placed the report in his desk. He would wait for the right moment to show it to his dad. Maybe this time his father would get excited about something good he'd done.

Chapter_2:
How to Teach—Character

How to Teach This

Here is a sample information bank for William Phillips, age fifteen.

- Dislikes creative writing, loves history
- Likes surfing the Internet, politics
- Hates scallops & oysters, loves lasagna
- Under his bed: vintage *Mad* magazines, hockey stick, his golden retriever's chew toy
- Bushy, sandy brown hair, brown eyes. 5'6", not muscular. Wears glasses to see the board
- Loves his three-year-old baby sister, dislikes his thirteen-year-old brother who always borrows his jazz CDs
- Favorite books: *War and Peace, Get Fuzzy*
- Likes to argue and debate, loses sometimes
- Wants to be a lawyer or Peace Corps worker
- Avoids flying. His cousin died in a plane crash.

Using "William's Information Bank," I could begin the paragraph:

> "William looked out the classroom window. He couldn't focus on his teacher at all."

Teaching the Story

The reader might wonder why William was distracted, but it is not a very exciting opening. By asking the class to use brainstormed details from the information bank, we could come up with:

> "William stared out the classroom window, his thoughts distracted. Usually he loved history class, but today he could care less about the Constitutional amendments."

That's a little better. Now the reader is going to want to know *why* William isn't interested in his favorite class. With class input I could write next,

> "Student council elections were tomorrow. He wasn't sure he was going to get elected as president."

That's interesting, but doesn't show any intensity of William's fears. Using students' suggestions, I could change that to read:

> "Student council elections were in less than twenty-four hours. William's stomach curled into a tight knot every time he thought about being pitted against Tiffany Johnson, his beautiful but incredibly blonde opponent.

Not bad. Now we have introduced some drama (the election is soon) and conflict (he's worried that he might not win). This also introduced William's "voice"—by calling Tiffany "incredibly blonde," the reader hears cynicism in his thoughts. Point out how some but not all of the information in the information bank was used.

For genre-specific **How to Teach This** examples, see the Chapter_2 folder on the Resource CD.

Create a Character—Make an Information Bank

- Character's name & age:
- Where does this person live? (city, country, castle, boarding house, army camp)
- How many brothers/sisters does he have? Who does he live with?
- What religion? Parents'/grandparents' nationalities? Race?
- Likes/Dislikes:

> Food
>
> Relative
>
> Famous person
>
> Hobby/leisure activity
>
> Sport
>
> People who...
>
> Book
>
> School subject
>
> Animal
>
> Type of clothes. Why?

Hint: *What your character* dislikes *may show more than what he likes.*

Background:

- What was the most important thing that happened to your character when he was little? What was his favorite toy?
- What is this person's most irritating habit? Why? What is different about him? What does his closet look like? Under his bed? What posters are on his wall?
- What does he think about most? What are his dreams? His secrets? What embarrasses him the most?
- What is the one thing in the world your character would do anything to avoid? Why? What has he already done to avoid it?
- What is the one thing your character wants more than anything else? Why? What has he already done to try to obtain it? What will he try in the future?
- Who is your character's enemy?
- What is your character's biggest weakness or flaw?

Teaching the Story

Describe Your Character

Person to be described:

Size (As tall/short as):

Weight (As skinny/heavy as):

Facial features:

    1. hair color, style, shape:

    2. eye color & shape:

    3. complexion:

    4. glasses? contacts? braces?

    5. distinguishing facial details:

Clothing:

    1. general style & fit:

    2. color, textures, preferences:

Accessories:

    1. jewelry—type and how much:

    2. other (shoes, boots, belts, hats, scarves, purses, etc):

Noticeable body features:

    1. hands and arms:

    2. legs and feet:

    3. torso:

    4. posture:

    5. unusual or distinctive traits:

You're Going to Name Him What?

Goal

To encourage students to think about the emotional impact of names and to brainstorm possible names for their characters.

Teacher Preparation

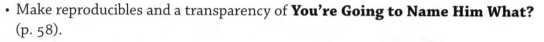

Chapter_2:
Name Him What

- Make reproducibles and a transparency of **You're Going to Name Him What?** (p. 58).

- Bring several phonebooks, newspapers, magazines, and a baby name book to class.

Instructional Tasks

In *Romeo and Juliet,* Juliet proclaims "What's in a name? That which we call a rose, by any other name would smell as sweet." Juliet's protests aside, names are important. Ask students to consider what they think of when they hear the following names:

Katerina Baronitsky	Doc Holliday
Gatsby Clark	Abraham Rosen
Raj Patel	Nick Roosevelt, Jr.
Scarlett Charleston	Chi Kan-Davis
Phil Rodriguez	Azza Arafat
Blanche O'Riley	Antonio Guiseppe

A character's name will trigger images in the reader's mind. Here are some hints:

- Harsh consonants convey feelings of strength. Examples: Jack, Rhett, Rackman.

- Soft vowels create a gentler image. Examples: Michelle, Susannah, Sloan.

- Names can reflect time period, locale, social status, culture.

Suggest that students make sure that their characters' names begin with different letters. Too many *Miriams, Marys,* and *Margarets* are confusing to the reader. Similarly, vary the length of the names that you use: naming characters *Bob, Sue,* and *Tom* is dull and doesn't grab the reader's attention.

Students should avoid using the exact name of friends or relatives. Besides getting them into trouble with the "real" person, they will be too tempted to describe the person they know rather than create someone new.

Using newspapers, magazines, phone books, or baby name books, students can brainstorm different name combinations.

Review **You're Going to Name Him What?**

You're Going to Name Him What?

To pick an appropriate name, consider the following:

DOES YOUR STORY TAKE PLACE NOW?

Look in the phone book or newspaper for possibilities. Avoid copying someone's real name by mixing up first and last names. Leaf through a baby name book (at your grocery store checkout counter) or look up baby names on the Internet.

DOES YOUR STORY TAKE PLACE IN THE FUTURE?

You can use a current name and add an unusual beginning or ending. In this way, Klein becomes *Kleinoid*, Smith becomes *Smithing*, and Davis becomes *Mongdavis*.

DOES YOUR STORY TAKE PLACE IN AMERICAN HISTORY?

Walk through a cemetery, read obituaries, look at historical websites.

DOES YOUR STORY TAKE PLACE IN MEDIEVAL TIMES, OR IS IT A MEDIEVAL FANTASY?

Browse medieval websites.

DOES YOUR STORY TAKE PLACE IN A FOREIGN LOCALE?

You may get some names from your local phone book or search the Internet. (Typing "name + generator" into any Internet search engine will lead you to several websites that generate unusual names.)

Mini-lesson

Suggested lesson length: 45 to 60 minutes

Meet the Bad Guy

Goals

- Teach the concept of *antagonist* and how he functions in a plot.
- Create an information bank for an antagonist.
- Model writing a descriptive paragraph about an antagonist.

Teacher Preparation

Have extra **Create a Character** and **Describe Your Character** worksheets available.

Instructional Tasks

Discuss how the antagonist is the person (or thing) which stands in the way of the main character (the protagonist) getting what he wants. If William wants to win the student council election, then Tiffany Johnson, his opponent, is his antagonist. If Theodore has lost his dog (or unicorn, spaceship, palomino pony, etc.) in a bad storm, then the storm is his antagonist.

The antagonist plays an important role in the story. By defeating the antagonist (or learning to live with defeat), the main character changes and matures. In a mystery, the antagonist's job is to try and prevent the main character (the protagonist/detective) from solving the mystery.

There are three questions to ask when developing an antagonist.

1. Why does she want to block the main character's goals? What is her motivation? Jealousy? Revenge? Anger? Saving herself?

2. How is she going to prevent the main character from getting what he wants?

3. What is the "chink" in her armor that will cause her own downfall? Will it be pride? Over-confidence? Impatience? Greed? Stupidity?

Answering these questions helps a writer develop his plot. The best stories show a main character that grows. One way to grow up is by cleverly outsmarting the bad guy.

In the same way that the main character should not be perfect, discuss how the antagonist should not be totally "evil." If it turns out that Tiffany Johnson tutors little kids after school every day, then it is harder for William to hate her. If the storm also provided rain for his father's drought-stricken farm, then Theodore will have many mixed feelings as he struggles to find his dog.

Following the example in the **Create a Character Information Bank** mini-lesson, brainstorm an antagonist with the class. You will probably have potential plot ideas floating around the classroom based on the protagonist that the students brainstormed. Choose one of these and create a person (or thing) that would keep the character from getting what he wants.

Model writing a descriptive paragraph about this character. What key detail should you include in order to portray this character's personality? If you prefer, you can begin the paragraph on the board, ask students to complete the paragraph on their own, and then have students read their paragraphs to the class.

Remind students who are writing a genre story that the details they choose to bring their antagonists to life must be consistent with their genres.

Looking Ahead

For homework, have students use **Create a Character** and **Describe Your Character** to create an information bank for their antagonist.

Students should write a four- to eight-sentence descriptive paragraph that uses information from their bank. Remind them that this is not the time to write the story but rather to get to know their characters. Encourage students to save plot ideas in their binder.

Chapter_2:
How to Teach—
Antagonist

How to Teach This

Here is a sample information bank for Brittany, who will serve as the antagonist for a character named Diedre:

- Brittany, thirteen, wears her black hair in long, tight braids, classy dresser
- Best friend is Diedre, but they argue at least once a week
- Mocking brown eyes
- Secretive
- Bossy, but other kids look up to her
- Best basketball player on the team

- Lives with her mother, step-father, and two younger step-brothers in a house in the suburbs.
- Likes history
- Refuses to eat meat

I could write this first sentence:

"Brittany is the best basketball player on the team."

That's a pretty boring sentence and simply repeats the information bank. With student input I could revise it:

"Whenever Brittany ran onto the basketball court, the crowd cheered."

By seeing the reaction of the crowd, we find out that Brittany is a good basketball player. But how are we going to show her mean side? The next sentence could read

"The other players loved having her on their team, but Diedre was her only close friend."

This is getting more interesting. Why doesn't Brittany have many friends? The next sentence could answer that.

"Her eyes always seemed to mock other people."

That's good, but is there a way to communicate additional information about Brittany's personality?

"Her deep brown eyes always seemed to say, 'I've got a secret that you don't know.'"

Now we're showing more about Brittany and paving the way for some conflict. What else could we use from the information bank?

"She always seemed to get her way with the team."

Always seemed is redundant from the previous sentence. Is there a way I could *show* Brittany and not just *tell* about her? Let's try,

"She wasn't exactly what you would call a bully, but Diedre never could say 'no' to her."

Now we've really painted a word picture of Diedre's antagonist.

For another example, see **Take it From the Bank—Create a Fantasy Antagonist** on the Resource CD.

Chapter_2:
Bank—Fantasy Antagonist

Suggested lesson length: 20 to 30 minutes

Dialogue

Goal

To expose students to some basic principles of writing dialogue and provide practice.

Teacher Preparation

Chapter_2:
How Does This Sound
Dialogue Tips
Give Em a Fight
Said This Better
Dialogue or Not

- Make transparencies and reproducibles of **How Does This Sound? Dialogue Examples from Literature** (p. 64), **Tips for Writing Dialogue** (p. 65), **Give 'em a Fight!** (p. 66), and **I Couldn't Have Said This Better Myself** (p. 67).
- Make copies of **To Dialogue or Not to Dialogue, That Is the Question** for students who are writing historical fiction.

Instructional Tasks

Ask students to read a small section of dialogue from their self-selected reading or use **How Does This Sound? Dialogue Examples from Literature**. Discuss how the author uses dialogue to show the reader more about who the character is while moving the story along.

Review **Tips for Writing Dialogue** and **Give 'em a Fight**.

Using class input, write several lines of dialogue between the character and the antagonist which the class brainstormed. Remind students to include information about what the characters are doing while they are talking. After four to six lines, direct students to continue writing the dialogue on their own. After ten minutes, ask students to read some of their examples.

If a student seems stuck, ask him to imagine what he would say if he were in the situation. Begin with that.

Hand out **I Couldn't Have Said This Better Myself** for students to refer to when practicing writing dialogue.

Teaching the Story

Extension

For more practice, ask students to give one of their brainstormed characters one of the following problems:

flunked an important test	got cut from the team
forgot her homework	late to get somewhere important
father/mother got fired	lost a friend's ring
family has to move	best friend lied

Write eight lines of dialogue between the character and an antagonist using at least ten to twenty words for each line.

Tip: *If the dialogue isn't strong, there is probably not enough conflict in the story between the two main characters.*

Looking Ahead

For homework, students should create eight to twelve lines of dialogue for their two main characters. This dialogue may or may not be used in the final story, but it brings the characters to life.

How Does This Sound?
Dialogue Examples from Literature

Finally, Crane-man poked him. "What demon scratches under your skin tonight?" he asked crossly. "It seems intent on keeping us both from slumber."

Tree-ear sat up, pulled his knees close, and wrapped his arms around them for warmth. "A question-demon," he said.

Crane-man sat up too. "Well, let us hear it, then. Perhaps if the question is asked and answered, the demon will leave you in peace—and I will be able to sleep."

Tree-ear answered slowly. "It is a question about stealing." He paused, started to speak, stopped again. Finally, "Is it stealing to take from another something that cannot be held in your hands?"

A Single Shard by Linda Sue Park
(Random House, 2001)

~~~~~~

"Let me tell you what happened. Please!"

It was just noise to him. A mask cannot hear. He kept coming toward me. I propelled myself through the tight little branches. From across the protecting hedge he commanded, "Come here this instant!" At his temple a vein was pulsating like a neon sign.

"Please give me a chance to explain. It was an accident," I said. "I was aiming at the hubcaps."

"He pointed a single quivering finger at me. "If you don't come here this instant I'll give you a beating you're never going to forget."

Did that mean if I came willingly he wouldn't hurt me? His face showed no sign of a thaw. Then I felt the warming spirit of Ruth. "The Lord gonna protect all His children." Fingers crossed, I stepped through the opening in the hedge to stand soldier-straight before my father.

~~~~~~~~~~

"I'll teach you to throw rocks at people!" he shouted, whipping the belt backwards through space.

"Nooo-ohhh! Please!" I begged. Can't stand more—can't.

Summer of My German Soldier by Bette Greene
(Penguin/Puffin Books, 1973)

Tips for Writing Dialogue

- Know your characters well. The best dialogue will come out of their personalities. Try to speak in their words. Vary lengths of sentences and use contractions. Listen to your family and friends. How do people *really* speak?

- Don't use dialogue unless it moves your story further along. Avoid mundane exchanges:

    Don't:

    "Hello," said Barbara.

    "Hello," answered Jerry.

    "How are you?" asked Barbara.

    "I'm OK," Jerry replied. "How about yourself?"

    This dialogue is as empty as the characters themselves.

    Try Instead:

    Barbara and Jerry slunk into the room at the same time. "Hi," Barbara offered tentatively. "You look better." Her hands were sweaty and her mouth felt like it was full of sand. They hadn't seen each other for ten months. What would this first meeting be like?

- Show your characters *doing something* as they talk. Is he shoveling grits into his mouth? Is she painting her toenails deep purple? Is the old man wiping his bifocals with an embroidered handkerchief? Does the teenager frown/roll her eyes/tremble/avert her eyes/giggle? Is the lawyer tapping his foot/pencil/briefcase impatiently? Gestures, body language, actions, and small habits can all add to the picture you create in your reader's mind.

- Show your characters' feelings through their words and the verbs you use, not by the way you attribute their dialogue. Most of the time you'll use *said* and *asked* to attribute a character's speech. But occasionally you can use words like *exclaimed*, *rejoiced*, *shouted*, *cried*, *explained*, or *interrupted*.

Give 'Em a Fight

What better way to see your characters' personalities than by letting them disagree?

Consider

- With whom does your character fight? What is the most probable cause?
- With whom does she refuse to fight? Why not?
- Does he fight physically, verbally, abusively, or in some combination of these?
- Does your character sulk, retreat, lash back, blame the other person, give in, act hurt, try to control the situation, seethe in silence, or try to undermine the other person?
- When things go wrong for your main character, what does she do? Does she rise to the challenge or shy away until the storm passes over?
- Does your character look for fights where none exist? Does he provoke disagreements by his hostile attitude?
- Is your character a peacemaker always trying to mend peoples' disagreements?
- What cause makes your character so mad she has no choice but to fight for it?
- Does your character fight "fair" or does he use name-calling, sarcasm, threats, lies, and belittling?
- Does your character bicker, quarrel, scream, or throw things?

Remember

- Clearly show why your character is upset and what she stands to gain or lose by fighting.
- Keep your characters distinct by giving them different fighting styles.
- Make sure a character's fighting style fits the type of person you have already created.

I Couldn't Have Said This Better Myself

Some Dialogue Hazards to Avoid

- Too much faithfulness to speech: "Um, uh, y'know, geez, well, like, well."
- Unusual spellings: "Yeah," not "Yeh" or "Yea" or "Ya."
- Too much variation: "he averred," "she riposted."
- Dialect exaggeration: "These bleedin' fings are 'eavy and I'm well on to workin' as 'ard as I can."
- Excessive direct address:

  "Tell me, Marshall, your opinion of Vanessa."

  "I rather hate her, Roger."

  "Why is that, Marshall?"

  "She bullies everyone, Roger."

Remember

- Each new speaker requires a new paragraph, properly indented and set off by quotation marks.

  "Use double quotations," the novelist ordered, "and remember to place commas and periods inside those quotation marks."

  "If a speaker goes on for more than one paragraph," the count responded in his heavy Transylvanian accent, "do not close off the quotation marks at the end of the first paragraph.

  "Simply place quotation marks at the beginning of the next paragraph, and carry on to the end of the quotation."

- Speak your dialogue out loud. If it doesn't sound natural, or contains unexpected rhymes and rhythms, revise it.
- If you are giving your characters' exact unspoken thoughts, do not use quotes or say, "he thought to himself." Both are unnecessary: simply paraphrasing your character's thoughts works best. A character's exact unspoken thoughts can be italicized.

  Todd fidgeted with his paper. *Do I want Dad to see this grade?* It was a tough call.

Based on work by Crawford Killian. Used with permission.

3

Setting the Scene

This set of five mini-lessons answers the questions, "Where does your story take place?" and "What could happen here?" According to Bruce Coville, author of *My Teacher Is an Alien* and *The Unicorn Chronicles,* good settings engage at least three of the five senses. To help your students become more aware of the sensory information all around them, they will first learn to sharpen their senses.

Following the pattern in the character block of mini-lessons, your students will examine the *show, don't tell* principle as it applies to setting. They will analyze samples from literature and other students to figure out what makes a setting become real to a reader. This lesson concludes with an activity which practices this important concept.

Your students will then be ready to create an information bank and brainstorm a setting in class as a precursor to creating a setting for their own story. You will again emphasize the importance of including specific details. Students will practice writing descriptive paragraphs about a setting.

The last two mini-lessons will help students apply these concepts. Students will learn how to use descriptive language to establish a mood. They will also learn how to use both character and setting to grab their readers' attention and launch their stories with oomph and pizzazz.

Sharpen Your Senses

Goal

To get students to include sensory data in their settings.

Teacher Preparation

Write down a number of different settings (*polar cap*, *crowded beach*, *the desert*, *foggy valley*, *amusement park*, etc.) on small slips of paper. Fold them and put them into a hat.

Instructional Tasks

Divide the class into groups of three or four students. Each group picks a setting out of the hat. For three minutes groups brainstorm an information bank describing this setting. Emphasize using all five senses: sight, smell, taste, touch, and sound. Using everyone's input, and *without* telling the specific location, one student writes a descriptive paragraph about the setting. After five minutes, a student volunteer reads the paragraph out loud to the class, and their peers guess the setting and comment on the most descriptive words and phrases.

Ask students to describe a vacation scene to a partner *without* using visual clues. Can their partner guess the place that is being described? Discuss which word clues were the best.

Looking Ahead

Ask students to use sticky notes to mark sample paragraphs in which the author *shows* the setting to the reader.

Mini-lesson

Show, Don't Tell Your Setting

Goals

• Demonstrate to students how authors *show* the setting to their readers.

• Encourage students to think about the *show, don't tell* concept through in-class critiquing of student samples.

Teacher Preparation

• Write a quote from **Advice from the Experts** (in the Chapter_1 folder on the Resource CD) on the board.

• Using a book which the class has read, create a transparency that vividly *shows* a setting. If your class is writing a genre story, pick a paragraph from that genre.

• Make copies of the **Show, Don't Tell—Worksheet** (p. 74).

• Make a transparency of **Show, Don't Tell—Student Samples of Settings** (p. 73). Or make a transparency from one of the genre-specific examples from the Resource CD.

Chapter_3:
Setting Worksheet
Student Samples Setting

Instructional Tasks

SHOW, DON'T TELL FROM LITERATURE

Read the setting example you selected. If you made an overhead, ask students to identify the words and phrases which *show* the setting and establish a mood. Discuss how the author is *showing* the setting through key details and not *telling* about it in vague, general terms.

Invite students to read sample descriptive paragraphs from their self-selected novels or short stories. Encourage students to give feedback about which words and phrases best show the setting and foreshadow what conflict could occur there.

SHOW, DON'T TELL PRACTICE

Put **Show, Don't Tell—Student Samples of Settings** on the overhead. Ask students to decide what is wrong with the *telling* paragraphs and which words or phrases make the *showing* paragraphs better. (Note that the third example also demonstrates a nice weaving of both character and setting.)

Alternatively, cover up the *showing* paragraphs and ask students to rewrite the *telling* paragraphs. After five minutes, uncover the *showing* paragraphs and allow students to compare and discuss their answers.

If you prefer, use one of the genre examples found on the Resource CD.

Give out copies of the **Show, Don't Tell—Worksheet**. This can be started in class and continued for homework.

Chapter_3:
 Student Sports Settings
Student Historical Settings
Student Mysterious
  Settings

Show, Don't Tell—Student Samples of Settings

Telling Paragraphs:

Nicole and Jessica were home alone when they heard a noise from the attic. They decided to find out what it was.

Felicity loved being outdoors and hearing the birds sing. But the American Army was about to ruin that.

Felix had been in a Roman prison for fourteen years. It was raining outside.

Rewritten as *Showing* Paragraphs:

Nicole and Jessica were up in Jessica's room when they heard a loud BANG from right above them...Slowly and crouching, Nicole forced herself to go up to the attic. As they pulled down the stairs to the attic, they both peered into the lonely, dark room. Just as Jessica took her first step up the ladder she heard the loud BANG again. But this time it was spine-shriveling. (Lee P., 6th grade)

Felicity rolled down the soft grassy hill and ran to the meadow....The birds sang a cheerful song, waking up the meadow. The morning dew mixed with the smell of the roses, creating a lovely fragrance flowing in the morning air. The sky was a beautiful colored quilt laying just beneath the morning sun, which was climbing up the sky...Suddenly, a faint sound of drummers and pipers sounded. Felicity peeked at the American Army marching to the beat of the music, coming closer and closer. (Lisa S., 4th grade)

Felix grunted as he was shoved back into the cramped prison cell that had been his home for fourteen years. With a mocking laugh, Lurius, the jailer, slammed the door shut and left. Felix sighed wearily. He had gotten a thumbs-down, which meant he had to kill his foe. He ran a finger down the scar that crossed his right eye. In his first few years as a gladiator, he had been defeated several times, but the determination and vigor with which he fought had earned him a number of thumbs-ups. He ran his other hand against the smooth stones that formed one wall of his little room. The stones were wet. It must have been raining outside. Probably still was. He closed his eyes. Fourteen years. (Robert B., 8th grade)

Show, Don't Tell—Worksheet

Directions

Rewrite the following sentences so that the reader experiences the setting. Feel free to change verbs, add adjectives, add similes and metaphors, or even add a person to the sentence. If you are writing a genre story, insert genre-specific details. The only rule is that you can't change the meaning of the sentence. Have fun!

EXAMPLE:

Big trees lined an old street.

REWRITE:

Oaks with trunks as fat as truck tires fought for sunlight along the rolling road.

1. The chairs felt funny when Linda dusted them.

2. The cornfield was dead.

3. All Olivia could hear was the siren.

4. The water that surrounded Lindsey tasted funky.

5. Gas filled Solomon's nostrils.

6. From the plane, the trees looked pretty.

7. The snow tasted cold.

8. The cage inside the room smelled strange.

9. Leslie had planted flowers along the sidewalk.

10. Clouds filled the sky.

# Mini-lesson

Create a Setting Information Bank

Goals

- Model the process of brainstorming a setting by using a graphic organizer.

- Model writing a descriptive setting paragraph.

- Stress the importance of consistency and using key details when creating a setting.

- Discuss how ideas for plot and conflict may surface while brainstorming a setting.

Teacher Preparation

- Write Neal Shusterman's quote from **Advice from the Experts** (in the Chapter_1 folder on the Resource CD) on the board.

- Make a transparency and copies of **Set the Scene—Create an Information Bank** (p. 78).

- If you are teaching a genre story, make copies of the appropriate genre-specific hand-outs from the Resource CD.

Chapter_3:
Setting Information Bank

Instructional Tasks

Using **Set the Scene—Create an Information Bank**, brainstorm a setting with your students. Examples of aspects of the setting which they should include and space for the students' own sample sentences are provided. (This also can be filled in for homework.)

Using student input, create a setting information bank.

Encourage students to use specific nouns and adjectives, as well as similes and metaphors to create images. Write the students' ideas on the board and ask them to describe what can be heard, smelled, seen, felt, or tasted. All answers must be consistent with previous information. For example, one of Jupiter's frigidly cold moons can't also have a steamy jungle. Even fantasy settings must be believable within the world that the writer is creating.

Begin a descriptive paragraph on the board. (See **How to Teach This** below.) Explain to students that descriptive paragraphs should be like frames frozen from a movie, not a video of an entire event. Remind students that not every piece of information in the information bank will be used.

Using the corral example, discuss how conflict and plot ideas might surface while creating the character's setting. Have students add four to six sentences to the paragraph that was begun on the board. Using the brainstormed information bank, they elaborate on the scene by adding their own details.

Discuss how describing the scene through the character's eyes shows both the character and the setting. Ask students to consider how different characters will experience the same setting from different perspectives.

If your students are writing a genre story, you can use one of the genre-specific **Take It from the Bank** transparencies (see the Chapter_3 folder on the Resource CD) and show how to use an information bank to write a descriptive paragraph.

Looking Ahead

For homework, students use **Set the Scene—Create an Information Bank** to brainstorm a setting for their stories. Students should write a four- to eight-sentence descriptive paragraph for their stories using this information bank.

Ask students to use a sticky note to mark a mood-conveying paragraph in their self-selected novels. They should bring their books to the next class.

Tip: *If a student doesn't know how to begin, ask her to remember three details which set a real place apart in her memory. Specific places will generate more accurate descriptions.*

Chapter_3:
How to Teach—Setting

How to Teach This

Here is a sample information bank for a corral, which could be the setting for a historical story.

- the smell of horse manure
- horses kicking up dust
- a red kerchief tied to a post
- hear a blacksmith working
- bridles slung over the brown, weatherworn fence

- people yelling at horses
- wooden wagon wheels on the ground
- lassos hanging on the wall of the barn
- sky as blue as Indian turquoise

With class input, this is how I would use that information to write a descriptive paragraph:

> "The sound of people yelling at their horses covered the corral like a lasso holding a bull."

After writing that, we might change *people* to *cowboys* (more specific noun) and insert *angrily* before yelling. After asking the students for a better verb than *covered*, we could replace it with *circled*. Switching *holding* to *tightening* also strengthens the image. The revision would read

> "The sound of cowboys yelling angrily at their horses circled the corral like a lasso tightening on a bull."

Commenting on this developing mood, we could write the following sentences:

> "Even the horses seemed tense and easily excitable. Pawing at the ground, kicking up their heels, shaking their long manes, it was as if they could smell the tension in the air."

Ask your students if they know if horses really act like that when they are tense and excitable. Point out how writers need to research descriptions like these for accuracy.

See the Resource CD for genre-specific **How to Teach This** examples.

Set the Scene—Create an Information Bank

Think about if your setting. Is inside or outside? Are there any unusual shapes? Is it night or day? What season is it? What is the weather like? The temperature?

Example: Raindrop bubbles popped on the steamy pavement.

What can the main character see (objects, people, scenery)?

Example: Cracker crumbs covered the car seat like a fine layer of desert sand.

What can the main character hear (teenagers screaming, wind whistling, trees crashing)?

Example: The lonely trumpet stumbled over a few, solitary notes.

What can the main character smell (thick chocolate fudge, burnt steak, wet dog, hot bread)?

Example: Even after twenty-five years, Creighton could still smell the spicy hot peppers and Italian beef of his favorite Chicago sandwich shop.

What can the main character feel (rough, smooth, sandy, hairy, fuzzy, cold, sticky)?

Example: The dry grass crunched like burnt potato chips under Lydia's feet.

What can the main character taste (salty chips, spicy salsa, sour apple)?

Example: Tart raspberry ice cream swirled around Maity's tongue as she walked toward the beach.

What colors can the main character see (gray blue sky, yellowed lace, blackened trees)?

Example: Water-washed weeds lay flattened along the creek's edge.

Suggested lesson length: 20 to 30 minutes

Create a Mood

Goals

- Show your students how the setting will communicate a mood to their readers.
- Practice creating a scene with a mood.

Teacher Preparation

- Choose a paragraph from a novel to read in class that creates a mood and foreshadows conflict.
- Make copies and reproducibles of **How Moody is Your Setting?** (p. 80) and **What Could Happen Here?** (p. 81)

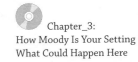

Chapter_3:
How Moody Is Your Setting
What Could Happen Here

Instructional Tasks

Review some student-selected examples of settings which show a mood. Refer back to the mini-lesson called **Sharpen Your Senses** and discuss which senses the author used to create that mood. Note how the setting foreshadows the story's conflict.

Assign small groups of students different moods such as *joyful*, *sad*, *peaceful*, *spooky*, *angry*, *worried*, *mysterious*, *menacing*, or *excited*. Each group takes ten minutes to develop a word list of nouns, verbs, and adjectives which show this mood. Then, using a familiar scene (like a snowstorm or the beach), ask every group to write about that setting in a way that conveys their emotion using as many words from their list as possible. Compare the results. Discuss how these different paragraphs could foreshadow different types of conflict.

Use **How Moody is Your Setting?** in class, or assign as homework. Students select a setting, brainstorm an information bank focusing on "moody" words, and then write a brief descriptive paragraph.

Tip: *Emphasize that the setting is the backdrop for the story. Ask students, "What do you want your reader to feel?" and "What adjectives, nouns, and verbs will prompt those feelings?"*

Looking Ahead

Hand out copies of **What Could Happen Here?** to fill in for homework.

How Moody is Your Setting?

Example Information Bank: Dark, quiet forest. Birds making strange noises, cold wind, ashes from a campfire.

Example of a Descriptive Paragraph: Daniel's footsteps sounded as loud as snare drums as he picked his way through the darkening forest. An owl's hoot startled him and he wondered again why he had taken Nathan's dare. Now he was lost and cold. Suddenly he could smell smoke. Across the way he could see a pile of glowing ambers. He wasn't the only one in the forest tonight.

Directions: Choose a setting and brainstorm a brief information bank. Write a short descriptive paragraph. Use specific nouns and active verbs as you write this paragraph. Don't forget to use some similes and metaphors too.

- A room where a scene from your story takes place. (Examples: attic, bedroom, basement, classroom, library, gym, bank office, principal's office). What is inside along the walls? What is hanging from the ceiling? What is stacked on the floor and desks? Is it dirty? Organized or messy? What type of furniture is there? Paintings? Accessories? Machines? What does it smell like? What can be heard in this room? What does your character feel as she enters this room? Why?

- A building where a scene from your story takes place (Examples: mall, house, abandoned shack, subway station, apartment building, airport, gym, store, school, trailer, police station, hospital). What is it made from? How many stories is it? What color is it? What does your character hear in this building? What does he see? What does he feel?

- What can your character see from a window? (Examples: empty parking lot, traffic in the street, kids playing in their yards, crowded pool, burned-down building.) What can your character hear? What does your character smell? How does this scene make him feel?

- An exterior setting where a scene from your story takes place (Examples: ocean, lake, dried-up river, desert, mountain top, snowy farm, street alley, forest, canyon). What colors does your character see? What can your character hear? Smell? Taste? Feel?

What Could Happen Here?

Directions: What is the developing mood in each example? How has the author communicated this mood? In the space provided, jot down ideas of what you think might happen next.

1. Fog settled over the mountain village like an old man settling into a long winter nap. Lori stared at her blank computer screen. There must be something she could do besides wait.

2. Screaming winds filled the bitter cold. Every lungful of air hurt. Ryan's boots slipped against the icy cliffs.

3. The arena was packed with sweaty spectators. Josh scanned the crowd, his stomach somersaulting over his breakfast. There was no room for error this time—his father had made that perfectly clear.

4. The room filled with the sounds of chairs scraping against linoleum and book bags thumping down. A throng of singing, joking, high-fiving students clattered into the room. Gladys Black surveyed the class and wondered if she would ever be ready for this challenge.

5. The roller coaster roared and music pumped through the speakers hidden in every other tree. Thick crowds pulsated through avenues stuffed with games and souvenir vendors. August's heat blared almost as loud as the merry-go-round.

Open Strong

Goals

• Recap both character and setting by showing how they need to be introduced quickly and in an interesting manner.

• Provide practice for writing strong openings.

Chapter_3:
Launch Your Story
Openings That Grab

Teacher Preparation

• Make copies of **Launch Your Story** (p. 84) and **Openings that Grab** (p. 85).

• Write the following quote on the board:

> "The opening scene needs to do five things: introduce your story's setting, introduce your story's major characters, begin to establish the emotional atmosphere, create some tension and suspense for what's to come, and introduce your story's major conflict. That's all."
>
> –Gloria Kempton

Instructional Tasks

Skilled writers grab their reader's attention as quickly as possible. Discuss with students how one common pitfall is including too much background information at the beginning. Writers need to start their stories with action and as close to the end of the story as possible.

Discuss the following as ways to get a story started:

• Set up questions in your reader's mind. ("Where is Carlos running to and why?")

• Show your character doing something that is interesting or potentially dangerous to themselves or the other character. ("Why in the world is Ashley getting into a strange car?")

• Show your character's strong emotions. This will often prompt the reader's questions. ("Why is Chris so mad? What happened?")

• Open with dialogue. ("Who in their right mind would say something like that in public?")

Hand out **Launch Your Story**. Each student picks two of the sentences to work on. After five minutes, hold an "Opening Challenge" contest. Read through the sentences and ask for volunteers to stand and read what they have written. Any student who thinks his sentence is more likely to get a reader's attention can challenge by standing and reading his. You decide which sentence is the most intriguing. The winner remains standing until a better one is read.

Hand out **Openings that Grab**. Encourage students to refer to it when writing their stories.

Looking Ahead

Students choose at least three other openings from **Launch Your Story** to work on. They can also rewrite the opening paragraph in **Openings that Grab** and insert conflict in it.

Launch Your Story

Directions: Rewrite the following sentences in a way that will grab your reader's attention and foreshadow some conflict. Use your imagination to add sensory information. Think about sights, smells, and sounds. Use vivid verbs, specific nouns, and expressive adjectives to show details. If you are writing a genre story, add genre-specific details.

1.   With her hands under her apron, Cassandra entered the large room.

2.   Ben walked down many steps leading downstairs into the basement.

3.   Something strange was coming out of the garage.

4.   Alexis wondered who had sent her the postcard.

5.   The shadows made Rachel feel uncomfortable.

6.   Bernardo felt something against his skin but he wasn't sure what it was.

7.   When Ashley opened the car door, a voice spoke to her.

8.   Marcus saw footprints leading into a cave.

9.   The message appeared once.

10. "You never believe me!" Pat said.

Openings That Grab

Dialogue—Between two important characters.

Setting—A short descriptive paragraph that shows your reader where and in what time period your story is taking place while setting the mood. Don't lose your reader by making this too long.

A vivid description of an important event—Past, present, or future.

The middle of an event—Show your character doing something. Let his or her actions tell the reader something important about himself or herself.

An interesting fact—Have one of your characters state alarming or unusual information to jumpstart your story.

Conflict—In the form of narrative or dialogue.

A cliffhanger—A hook to get your reader interested in your story.

Feelings—Show how your character feels in response to an important person or event.

FIX THIS OPENING PARAGRAPH:

The alarm clock woke Travis at the usual time. He hit the snooze alarm three times before he got out of bed. He pulled on his jeans and a T-shirt and brushed his hair. He could hear his sister singing in the bathroom. Her voice was so annoying! But that was only the smallest irritation at this point. Today he had to walk her to school and so he wouldn't be able to ride the bus with his friends.

Developing the Plot

In this block of mini-lessons, your students will identify the key problems that their characters will face and the obstacles that they'll meet in resolving them. Your job will be to encourage students to pick a problem that can be shown (not told) and resolved in 800-1600 words. This won't be easy! Middle-school students love to dream up problems of epic proportions. During the course of this unit, you have probably seen stories about the young girl whose horse runs away to the next state but is found just in time for the owner to win the blue ribbon at the state jumping competition. If you can limit the scope of your students' stories, their writing will be better and you won't have to be the bad guy saying over and over again, "No, your story can't be 6000 words long!"

Following the pattern in the other blocks, you and your students will first look at how to *show*, not *tell* the character's problem. You will look at examples from literature as well as a student sample.

In the second mini-lesson, the class will brainstorm different problems that are simple, believable, and solvable. Your students will also learn to boil problems down into one plot sentence.

In the **Build-a-Plot** mini-lesson, your students will practice outlining stories using this essential graphic organizer. They will then use this graphic organizer to outline their own story.

Plot Props is a quick, fun mini-lesson in which students use a word list to brainstorm a plot for a story.

The last mini-lesson, **Boy, It's Tense in Here!**, shows students how to increase conflict by adding more tension to their stories.

Show, Don't Tell Your Character's Problem

Goals

- Review the ways in which authors show their characters' problems **FAST**: through feelings, actions, speech, and thoughts.

- Prompt students to think about how to *show, don't tell* through in-class critiquing of a student sample and writing a brief descriptive paragraph.

Teacher Preparation

- Write the following quote on the board:

  "Plot is what happens when desire meets obstacles. A story is the protagonist struggling against difficult odds for a worthwhile goal. [It is about] who wants what and why he can't have it."

  –Bruce Coville

Chapter_4:
Bear Attack

- Make a transparency of **The Bear Attack** (p. 90).

- Select a portion of a novel which shows a main character's problem.

Instructional Tasks

Read a portion of a novel or ask students to read a selection from their self-selected novels or short stories. Discuss the words and phrases the author used to portray the character's conflict. Was the conflict also communicated through the mood of the setting? Discuss the interrelationship of the three main story elements: character, setting, and plot.

Put **The Bear Attack** on the overhead and lead a discussion about what is wrong with it. Although it is descriptive, the author simply lists the events and *tells* the story. For example, when the bear attacks, the author could have written, "Joey's eyes and stomach filled with cement-like fear. He knew he could never escape those huge, sharp claws." Showing the events through the character's reactions connects the reader emotionally to the story. Ask the class how they could have shown the character's problem **FAST**.

Point out that the game warden, not Joey, solves the problem and that without appropriate paragraph breaks, the story *appears* long and uninteresting—the reader is not given any visual cues about changes in the action. Discuss where the writer could have inserted dialogue and how that would have enhanced the story.

Give one of the characters that the class brainstormed for a previous lesson one of the following problems:

- forgot to raise the drawbridge
- left the extra gas can for the fishing boat on the dock
- brought home a progress report with two failing grades
- left younger sister outside near the pool and went inside to answer the phone
- father discovers banned websites on character's computer
- best friend suddenly won't talk to her
- printer died the night before a report is due

In pairs or individually, students write a brief descriptive paragraph which shows this problem **FAST**.

The Bear Attack

by Jackson G.

One wintry cold foggy morning, Joey was hunting in the deep woods of South Carolina with his older brother Bobby. Joey's eyes were as dark as a brown bears' fur coat and he was as tall as a baby bear standing on his two feet. His skin was fair because he never got sun burned. Bobby was tall and strong. Bobby and Joey were checking their animal traps for raccoons because they left out bait. They catch lots of raccoons because the raccoons like the bait which is old, moldy cheese. They found three living raccoons in the traps. Ripper, their dog, chased a big fat squirrel up a tree. Joey saw a rabbit hop quickly into its hole. Ripper sniffed the ground and chased two big rabbits out of the hole.

———

Joey and Bobby hiked up to a waterfall about four miles from their cabin...When they got there they went fishing...They caught four big trout. They started a fire and cooked their fish. After they ate, they went hunting. About one or two miles from camp they walked close to a baby cub. They didn't want to make it mad so they walked past slowly and as quietly as a mouse. But then Ripper started barking at the bear. Big Momma came running out of the trees. The massive bear stood up on two legs and attacked Joey by scratching him with his sharp claws. Joey tried to stab the bear with his pocket knife. But the bear was too strong for Joey to pull off himself. Bobby couldn't shoot the bear off Joey either. He didn't want to miss and hurt Joey. A man suddenly came running through the trees. He stood right in front of the bear and aimed his big rifle at the bear's legs. The bullets hit the bear's legs and made him run away from Bobby, Joey and the man. Joey had cuts all over his body. Also, his clothes were turn up. Joey could walk fine and they decided to hike back to their camp. The man that helped them fight off the bear was a game warden and offered Joey and Bobby a ride back to their cabin. The man used his radio to call town and told them he was going back to town. The man dropped Joey and Bobby off at their cabin. They called their friends and asked them to come over so the could tell them what happened. All their friends were so astonished when they heard the terrible story. They were so amazed that Joey lived through it. They decided to go down to the diner in town for dinner. They were thankful that the man came and helped them out.

Teaching the Story

Mini-lesson

Suggested lesson length: 30 to 40 minutes

Plan-a-Problem

Goals

• Help students to brainstorm believable, simple problems.

• Teach students the concept of plot sentences and provide practice writing them.

Teacher Preparation

• Make copies and transparencies of **Plan-a-Problem** (p. 96), and transparencies of **Examples of Real Life Problems** (p. 94) and **Give Your Characters Problems They Can Handle** (p. 95).

• Write the following quote on the board:

> "If you stayed at home tonight and watched TV you would see the same story over and over again. I call it man-in-hole. But it needn't be about a man or a hole, just somebody who gets into trouble, gets out of it again. People love that story."
>
> –Kurt Vonnegut

Chapter_4:
Plan-a-Problem
Real Life Problems
Problems Characters Can
Handle

Instructional Tasks

Remind students that since the foundation of good stories consists of a *plausible* problem, they may need to do some research to find appropriate key details. (Refer back to the **Background Research** mini-lesson on page 35.) The character's conflict is the core of the story, key details are the icing on the cake that makes a story real to the reader.

On the overhead, brainstorm the types of conflicts which people face. You can use the **Plan-a-Problem** transparency and fill in examples from students' self-selected novels, or use the brainstormed characters and settings from the previous two lessons. Review how character and setting will already have suggested plot ideas. Note how full-length novels include many problems, but short stories usually focus on one main problem.

Following are some examples from popular young adult novels. See the Recommended Reading Lists (in the Chapter_1 folder of the Resource CD) for information on these books.

Person vs. Person(s): In *Catherine Called Birdy*, Catherine constantly fights her father about his choice of a husband for her. Janie Johnson's conflicts with her adoptive parents and "real family" in *The Face on the Milk Carton*. Sally Lockhart vs. the opium dealers in *The Ruby in the Smoke*.

Person vs. Self: Bilbo's doubts in *The Lord of the Rings*. In *Ghost Boy*, Harold struggles with accepting himself as an albino. Billy's struggles with his own fears and desires in *Where the Red Fern Grows*.

Person vs. Nature or Animal: Tim, Alexis, Dr. Alan Grant, & Dr. Ellie Sattler against the dinosaurs in *Jurassic Park*. In *The Yearling*, Jody faces a variety of struggles with his fawn, Flag.

Person vs. Society/Law: In *Roll of Thunder, Hear My Cry* the Logan family faces a number of conflicts with the white community. Jonas hates the utopian society in *The Giver*. Scout and Jem's contact with prejudice against blacks in the rural South in *To Kill a Mockingbird*. Stanley's conflict with the prison wardens as he struggles to find the truth in *Holes*.

Person vs. God or Uncontrollable Force: In *The Bronze Bow*, Daniel is upset with Jesus for not being the political Messiah he is expecting and for not fighting Rome. Winnie in *Tuck Everlasting* struggles against the power that is within the fountain of everlasting water. In *Hatchet*, Brian's struggles to survive when the plane he is traveling on crashes.

Person vs. Machine: In *The Grapes of Wrath*, the farmers are angry with the tractors which come in and rip up their fields and homes. Kel fights the killing machines in *Lady Knight*. The effect of the bomb on Japan as described in *Hiroshima*.

Use **Examples of Real Life Problems** or **Give Your Characters Problems They Can Handle** to discuss how students need to give their characters simple problems. Ask students to think about problems which they or their friends have faced and resolved. Many of these problems are universal and can occur in different settings and time periods. They should avoid choosing huge, unrealistic problems such as escaping a death threat from the mafia, being a CIA agent who protects the United States from a terrorist attack, rescuing the world from alien invasion, or saving an entire town from cholera. Have students review their **Getting to Know You—The Author** worksheets and look for problems that might be interesting to write about. Adding the question "What if?" can turn normal everyday events into story ideas.

Here are some examples of simple, limited problems that could be handled in a short story:

Person vs. Person(s): Wendy and her best friend Lauren are both trying out for the lead in the school play. The night before the audition, Wendy can't find her script.

Person vs. Self: Omarastan is afraid that if he doesn't master the next level of anti-gravity exercises, his friends will advance in the space academy without him.

Person vs. Nature or Animal: Sean is left in charge of a cow that may have difficulty birthing her calf. He falls asleep by the fire and when he wakes up, there is a blizzard outside.

Person vs. Society/Law: Lisa wants to play football but girls aren't allowed to play on the team.

Person vs. God or Uncontrollable Force: On the way to boarding the ship that will take him to America, Henry sees a Gestapo blockade. Will he get through before his boat leaves?

Person vs. Machine: Phillip's dirt bike chain has fallen off and the wire breaks in his clutch. Can he fix these in time to complete the big race?

Discuss the concept of plot sentence. Ask students to select one of the conflicts that you have discussed in class and summarize it using the following plot sentence:

This story is about _____, who more than anything wants to _____ but can't because _____.

Write several sample plot sentences with the class using characters which the class brainstormed.

Looking Ahead

For homework, students should fill out the **Plan-a-Problem** worksheet and write a plot sentence for their stories. Advise students that it might require several attempts before they are able to pinpoint the main conflict that their characters will face. When determining this conflict, students should ask themselves, is it possible for my character to solve this problem? The more they can narrow down their characters' problems, the more likely they will be able to *show*, not just *tell* it.

Examples of Real Life Problems

Person vs. Person(s): parent vs. child, siblings or best friends fighting, peer pressure at school, gossip, jealousy, teasing.

Person vs. Self: self-doubt over one's looks, grades, or athletic abilities; anger over wrong decision or indecisiveness; worry about making new friends after a move.

Person vs. Nature or Animal: encounter with a snake, a nest of hornets, an unfriendly dog, surviving a dark night alone in a forest, or a hail storm while camping.

Person vs. Society/Law: character caught shoplifting or cheating, character protesting a school rule.

Person vs. God or Uncontrollable Force: sickness keeps student from taking final exams, a fire destroys valuable family pictures and documents, a major snowstorm keeps character from making an important appointment.

Person vs. Machine: character loses data on a computer, character can't open an important lock, wheel on a covered wagon breaks along the Oregon Trail.

Give Your Characters Problems They Can Handle

If you are struggling to create a manageable problem for your character, think of scenes instead of entire stories. The more problems you give your character, the more difficult it will be to resolve them all appropriately. This is a short story, not a novel!

If you focus on a smaller, real-life conflict which you have encountered (jealousy and competition in a class, facing someone on the court who plays "dirty," watching a teammate stumble and fall while running cross-country) you will be less likely to have to resolve the story with a "magical," unrealistic ending. These stories may seem less dramatic, but they are easier to write.

If you are writing a genre story, make your character do "ordinary" things (such as try to get out of homework, fight with her siblings, hate chores, be tempted to cheat or lie) in a different environment. This makes the story more believable and enjoyable for you as a writer and your reader.

Tip: *Your reader should be able to identify with some aspect of your main character's conflict.*

Plan-a-Problem

Person vs. Person(s)

Person vs. Self

Person vs. Nature or Animal

Person vs. Society/Law

Person vs. God or Uncontrollable Force

Person vs. Machine

Think: *What is my character's problem? How is he going to solve it? What obstacles will my character meet along the way?*

Tips for writing your story:

• Choose one main problem for your 800-1600 word story.

• Focus on one incident—not a person's whole life.

• Avoid quick, "they-all-lived-happily-ever-after" solutions.

Teaching the Story

*Mini-lesson* —————————————————————————

Suggested lesson length: 20 to 30 minutes

Build-a-Plot

Goal

To help students develop a workable plot using a graphic organizer.

Teacher Preparation

Make a transparency and copies of **Build-a-Plot** (p. 100). If you are teaching a genre, pick one of the genre-specific versions in the Chapter_4 folder on Resource CD.

Chapter_4:
Build-a-Plot.pdf

Instructional Tasks

Remind students that a good plot includes the character wanting something that he has difficulty in achieving.

Put **Build-a-Plot** on the overhead. This outline will help them focus on a story with one or two main characters and settings which take place in a short period of time. Point out the following:

- The problem is in the middle of this graphic organizer because it is central to the construction of the story. Students should have clearly identified their characters' main problems in their plot sentences, which were written in the previous mini-lesson.

- Double arrows between the character, setting, and the problem indicate that they impact one another. For example, if Omarastan's story takes place in a space school, then he's not going to worry about helping to birth his father's calf. The character and setting will play a role in what the character's problem is and how he will resolve it. This in turn leads to the story's events.

- Not every story will have four events. Some may have fewer, but caution your students that more than four will probably make the story too long. Events are the answer to "What happens next?" They heighten the story's tension by throwing obstacles in the main character's path, and they move the story forward. Refer to a simple story (Little Red Riding Hood works well) to show how the character's problem (she had to take food to her sick grandmother) is intensified by complicating obstacles (the forest is dark, she meets a hungry wolf, etc.).

Chapter 4 | Developing the Plot

- The climax is when the character works through the obstacles in her path and makes a decision which enables her to obtain or not obtain her goal (the climax in *Little Red Riding Hood* is when she tricks the wolf.). This is usually the turning point of the story. The character needs to achieve this goal through her courage (physical, mental, or spiritual), ingenuity, or ability. All of the story's events should lead to this climax.

- The resolution is the end. If possible, it includes what the character has learned or how he has grown as a result.

- Encourage students to fill this out in pencil since they will probably revise it as they brainstorm and outline their stories.

Using the **Build-a-Plot** transparency, fill in the boxes for a sample story. You can use one of the characters and problems which your students brainstormed in class or one of the following examples. If your students are writing a genre story, use the appropriate genre-specific **Build-a-Plot** from the Resource CD.

EXAMPLE #1

More than anything else, Jason wants to be on the basketball team. His problem (person vs. self) is that he thinks he's not good enough. Despite his older brother teasing him that he'll never make it because he's too clumsy (Event #1), having difficulty scheduling practices because of extra school work as a result of bad grades (Events #2 & #3), Jason is determined to try out. Then, he finds out that his parents planned a surprise trip to Disney World during the long weekend when try-outs (Event #4) are being held. The climax, which is the turning point of the story, will be when Jason figures out how he can still try out for the team. The resolution, which brings the story to a satisfactory end, shows Jason either meeting his goal of getting on the team, or living with the disappointment of not getting on the team—whichever the author chooses.

EXAMPLE #2

Carolyn has lost her dog, Jazz, and more than anything else wants to find him. The story shows a series of events that prevent Carolyn from immediately finding Jazz. Does Carolyn suspect that Jazz was stolen? Does a snowstorm keep Carolyn from looking for him? Does she have to go to school and worry about him all day? Stress that students can't let their stories get mired in tangents: how Carolyn rescued Jazz as a puppy might be cute, but maybe it isn't necessary. Note the following:

- The problem should be simple, but the complications and events which prevent Carolyn from finding Jazz will make the story interesting.
- The climax of the story is Carolyn's pivotal decision or action which leads her to finding Jazz (or not finding him.) Not all stories have a happy ending.

Tip: *Encourage students to have their characters act, not just think about their problem.*

Tip: *Students should avoid creating miraculous endings.*

Looking Ahead

If they haven't already done so, students should complete their **Build-a-Plot**, **Plan-a-Problem**, and plot sentence.

Extension

Have each student select a partner. Together they think of a role-playing situation that would demonstrate one of the problems which the class brainstormed. Taking two to three minutes, they role-play this in front of the class. The rest of the class writes a three- to five-sentence description of what they have seen and takes turns reading this paragraph out loud. Point out how the same situation is often described in different ways. These paragraphs are a summary of the action, rather than the story itself.

Build-a-Plot

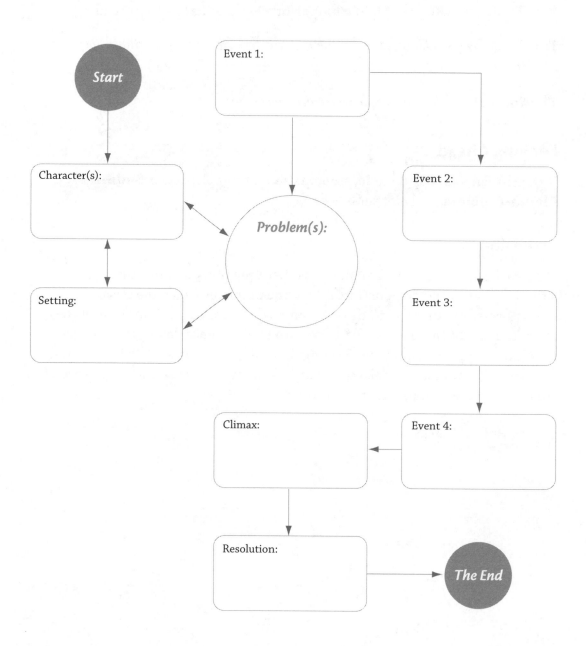

Mini-lesson

Suggested lesson length: 30 to 40 minutes

Plot Props

Goal

Demonstrate how a story can begin with a list of props.

Teacher Preparation

Print **Plot Props** off the Resource CD. (The file on the CD is formatted one list per page so you can easily print and distribute the lists to your student groups.)

Chapter_4 :
Plot Props

Instructional Tasks

Divide the class into small groups and hand each one a **Plot Props** list. Each group has fifteen to twenty minutes to write a mini-story that includes each word on their list. They may add adjectives—*dried* blood—if they need to.

To encourage each group to keep the story moving, impose a time limit on the action: characters only have a total of thirty minutes from the beginning to the end of the story.

One student records the eight- to twelve-sentence story. Afterwards, ask a representative from each group to read the story. The class may vote on which story is the best. After the stories are read, highlight the story elements which the writers included, such as the character, antagonist, setting, and problem. Discuss how these simple, fast stories often are outlined and told, rather than shown.

Extension

Ask your students to come up with their own plot prop list and mini-story. If they get stuck, they can get ideas from a newspaper or magazine.

Plot Props

PROP GROUP 1
blood
punctured bike tire
torn woolen sweater
rusty nail
leather boot

PROP GROUP 2
spaceship door jammed
climate control broken
explosive noise
darkness
broken leg

PROP GROUP 3
torn photograph
locked trunk
journal
creaky stairs
wig

PROP GROUP 4
senator
stolen passport
jet
security gate
computer

PROP GROUP 5
blackened wood
ashes
horse
prize ribbon
horseshoe

PROP GROUP 6
Internet
strange message
sticky note
science project
grade

PROP GROUP 7
phone call
kitchen
mother
baby crying
package

PROP GROUP 8
deflated basketball
torn net
footprint in cement
gray tracks
painted message

PROP GROUP 9
strong winds, hail
torn sail
chains clanking
barrels rolling on deck
lighthouse beam

PROP GROUP 10
robots
huge factory
intercom
bloody rags
laser gun

PROP GROUP 11
pick and hammer
dirty boots
pistol
black horse, dusty tack
cavern

PROP GROUP 12
dried herbs
jeweled sword
cauldron
black forest
broken wheel

PROP GROUP 13
hot wind
shack with a tin roof
empty water barrel
corn stalks
skinny gray cat

PLOT GROUP 14
clock moving backwards
smell of incense
scampering noise
curtains blowing out a window
total eclipse

 # Mini-lesson

Boy, It's Tense in Here!

Goal

Help students consider ways to make their stories more interesting and suspenseful.

Teacher Preparation

• Write the following quote on the board:

> "Think about the worst things that could happen to a character in this situation. Make them happen."
>
> –Theodore Scott Bell

• Make copies and a transparency of **Let's Up the Ante** (p. 104).

Chapter_4:
Up the Ante

Instructional Tasks

Hand out copies of **Let's Up the Ante** and discuss. Using the **Build-a-Plot** transparency, review the story which the class created and discuss ways it could be made more suspenseful. Decide which events are the most significant and should be emphasized.

Ask students to review their **Build-a-Plots** and consider whether or not they can insert more tension into one of the events. This activity can also be done in pairs so that students hear a peer's input.

Tip: *Forcing a character to make tough choices will create tension and keep the reader hooked, as well as show more about the character's personality.*

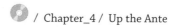

Let's Up the Ante
(Or, How to Keep Your Reader Hooked)

Make sure that the event is worth getting tense about. Not fixing her hair perfectly isn't a big deal unless Brooke woke up late, got to school late, and is supposed to give a speech in front of the entire school for the upcoming student government election.

Get your character into physical trouble. Crossing the street shouldn't be a dangerous experience unless there are buses, trucks, and cars speeding at over 60 mph and Bonita must reach the other side in order to get to her little sister.

Get your character in trouble with another person. Has Julie lied, gossiped, or deceived her best friend? Is she embarrassed to admit what she's done?

Add a time limit. Neil has to get home by 11 p.m. or else be grounded for a month. He gets a flat tire on the way...will he make it on time?

Tie characters together. Not literally, but if Kathryn can't prevent Michael, whom she is babysitting, from stepping onto a pond covered with very thin ice because she is running after Michael's younger brother Patrick, then Kathryn and Michael are both in trouble.

Make the unknown scary. If Kevin has to fly to visit grandparents who he has never met and yesterday there was a major airline disaster...then he might be wondering what's in store for him.

5

Writing the First Draft

Your students are now ready to assemble the building blocks of their stories. They should be like runners at the starting line—excited and ready to start the race.

As I have alluded to throughout this unit, stories aren't like the building-block towers that your students built as children—one block doesn't just rest on the one below it. Instead, the character, setting, and plot components will dynamically influence each other while the author writes the story. Changes at this stage are not only numerous, but they are also necessary. It is not uncommon for students to find out that the character which they originally imagined no longer fits the setting or problem. Or visa-versa. Often, if she hasn't carefully defined her character's problem, a writer might find she has written five pages but still hasn't gotten to the problem which is *really* important and those first five pages have to be (gulp!) crumpled up and thrown away. You can temper the reluctance to cut this writing by encouraging students to save it in their binders for possible use in future writing projects.

These are the challenges which your students will discover and tackle during this writing block. All of the mini-lessons are short so that most of the class time can be devoted to writing. This also allows time for you to conference with students.

If students have access to computers, encourage them to begin typing their stories as soon as possible. This eliminates illegibility and expedites the revision process. Rewriting and editing is accomplished quicker if it can be done electronically.

Keep in mind that some students use and merge the story elements which they have already created. Others might want to start all over using the tools which this unit has provided. Your schedule will most likely dictate what you can allow. If you are using this unit over the span of a month or more, then your students might have the time and luxury to start a story, trash it, and start a new one. Clearly communicate the students' deadlines so they can make informed decisions. Work can also be done at home. Allow at least three days for students to complete the goal of this block of mini-lessons: a double-spaced rough draft which you and their peers will read and critique.

Mini-lessons include **Put It All Together**, **Make the Transition**, **Write a Short Story—Not a Novel**, **Get Un-Stuck**, and **Your Title Here**. The last mini-lesson—**"The End"**—will help your students resolve their stories without supernatural or adult intervention. Middle-school students love the drama of the underdog hockey player winning the game as the buzzer sounds or the cheerleader who is dropped, suffers a concussion, and is "miraculously" healed before the national competition. Unfortunately, these stories aren't very believable. This lesson will help them avoid common mistakes while writing the endings to their stories.

Remember, use the lessons which your students need and feel free to combine two mini-lessons as appropriate.

Put It All Together

Goal

Students will begin writing their rough drafts using their information banks, plot sentences, and **Build-a-Plots**.

Teacher Preparation

None.

Instructional Task

Discuss how the ingredients for a cake or the parts of a house are individually important, but when put together they produce a separate entity. Similarly, blending the separate story elements together will create a product that is greater than the sum of its parts. Experienced writers weave together information about the main character and the setting by showing the character's feelings, actions, speech, or thoughts. Consider the following opening paragraphs:

> "You've got to be kidding!" Mitchell looked up from his laptop and looked at his younger brother with eyes that could have melted the screensaver right off of the computer. [speech, action] "Jason, you'll never make East Meck's basketball team. Look at you! You're a clumsy turd. Just because you played in that rec league doesn't mean you're good enough for a high school JV team!" [provides information about Jason and Mitchell. Sets up the conflict.]
>
> Jason clenched his teeth and looked down. [feelings, action] He was tired of Mitchell always acting as if he knew everything. He was tired of being made fun of and tired of feeling like a giraffe with six feet that get tangled up every time he walked through the gym door. [thoughts, feelings] Without a word, Jason stamped out of his brother's room. [action] Team tryouts were in a month. He'd show him. [thoughts which show self-doubts and set up story's problem.]

Tip: *Warn students not to dump their information banks or paragraphs into big lumpy passages—instead, they should weave this information into the fabric of their stories.*

Tip: *Some students will appear to finish their rough drafts quickly. Frequently these students are hurrying up to finish the assignment and have told and not shown their stories. Mention this and suggest that they begin the self-editing process using the* **FMEs—Frequently Made Errors** *(p. 124) reproducible from Chapter 6.*

Tip: *Review your students' plot sentences. This will help you spot unoriginal characters or problems that are too big.*

Mini-lesson

Make the Transition

Goal

Help students incorporate appropriate transitions.

Teacher Preparation

Make an overhead and copies of **Useful Transitions** (p. 110).

Chapter_5:
Useful Transitions

Instructional Task

Put Useful Transitions on the overhead. Discuss how writers need to get their characters from one point in time or place to another. How do you get Jason out of his house and onto the basketball court? Do you have to show him getting out of bed, getting dressed, driving to the gym and arriving at practice? Probably not. Authors select the events and details which move the story along.

One of the most convenient ways to transition from one event to another is to show the passage of time. A student could write, "The next day after school, Jason was in the gym five minutes after the last bell rang." The reader knows one day has passed, sees Jason's determination, and is ready for the next event. Or the author could write, "After three weeks of practice, Jason felt ready." Either way, the writer moves the story along through the passage of time.

- Good transitions between paragraphs will make sure that the story flows and makes sense.

- Good transitions will show the character acting, without the reader having to see each place he stopped along the way.

- Dialogue can also be used as a transition between paragraphs.

- Writers should avoid event lists (refer back to **The Bear Attack** on page 90.)

Useful Transitions

Transitions which can be used to **show location**:

Above	By
Across	Down
Against	In back of
Along	In front of
Alongside	Inside
Among	Into
Around	Near
Away from	Off
Behind	Onto
Below	On top of
Beneath	Outside
Beside	Over
Between	Throughout
Beyond	Under

Transitions which can be used to **show time**:

About	Next
After	Next week
Afterward	Previously
As soon as	Second
At	Soon
Before	Then
During	Third
Finally	Today
First	Tomorrow
Immediately	Until
In the meantime	When
Later	Yesterday
Meanwhile	

Mini-lesson

Suggested lesson length: 15 to 20 minutes

Write a Short Story—Not a Novel

Goal

Help students limit the scope of their stories.

Teacher Preparation

Make a transparency of **Write a Short Story—Not a Novel** (p. 112).

Chapter_5:
Not a Novel

Instructional Task

Put **Write a Short Story—Not a Novel** on the overhead and discuss the quote and the points below.

Tip: *Warn students not to moralize. If they want their characters to learn a "lesson," make sure it is integrated into the story.*

Write a Short Story—Not a Novel

"A short story can waste no words. It may recount only one central action and one major change or effect in the life of the central character(s). It can afford no digression that doesn't directly affect the action. A short story strives for a single emotional impact, imparts a single understanding. A good short story is tight, sharp, economic, well knit, and charged. A short story requires a conflict, a crisis, and a resolution."

–Robin Nobles

- Background information is just that, information that stays in the background and is needed only as the reader needs it. Like the information bank, you will draw from it when writing your story.
    ◊ Start with your character in the middle of action.
    ◊ Don't start with a descriptive paragraph about what happened before the story begins.
- Don't write about the character's whole life, just the part that is relevant to her current predicament.
- Don't get "bunny trailed" off onto secondary characters or plots (the main character's best friend who also wanted to compete in the 5K but couldn't because his brother was injured in a motorcycle accident). Stay focused on the main character's problem.

What *not* to write

Tom White has dreamed of playing in the Stanley Cup finals ever since he was a boy. When his team finally makes it, his plane is hijacked by terrorists and then crashes on a deserted island. Tom is kidnapped by robbers, but a volcano erupts and kills the kidnappers. After fighting off wild animals and facing starvation, Tom is rescued off the island by a Russian boat that happens to be in the area, and the Russians get him to the game on time.

Mini-lesson

Get Unstuck

Goal

Provide strategies that "stuck" students can use to move forward.

Teacher Preparation

None.

Instructional Tasks

Like adult authors, student writers sometimes feel stuck. Their stories might jump from the starting line with great enthusiasm and wonderful descriptions but lose momentum somewhere after the first page. Or, claiming writer's block, students complain that they don't know what to write next.

Review the following strategies with your students:

- **Start as close to the problem as possible.** Opening with a character's action, or reaction to an event or person, hooks the reader's attention. Too often novice writers begin with boring background (i.e., family history, events which happened before the story takes place, a detailed physical description of the setting or character) that is necessary for them to know as the writer but is not interesting to the reader. (Review **Openings that Grab**, p. 85.)

- **Reread the plot sentence.** What is the main character's goal? What will he do to get what he wants, and what events will prevent him from reaching his goal? Prompting the student to imagine that he is the character also helps. Asking, "What would you say?" or "What would you do next?" may help the student move on.

- **Review Build-a-Plot.** Has the student stayed with the problems which she had planned for her character, or is the character off on a new "bunny trail" that has nothing to do with the main plot of the story? If the student changes her story, she should fill out a new Build-a-Plot. This is the best tool to help her think sequentially about the story and bring it to a logical conclusion.

- **Break the task into small pieces.** Some students will feel overwhelmed by the thought of writing an entire story. Focusing on each separate event should help them move beyond a blank piece of notebook paper. Encourage students to give their characters one main problem. (How was Little Red Riding Hood going to get to Grandma's house?) Remind them that brief is better.

- **Don't worry about getting it perfect…yet.** Some students get stuck writing and rewriting their first paragraph trying to get everything perfect. Encourage your students to turn off their internal editors and to enjoy the process of writing. Editing and revising will come later. (There's a good chance that first paragraph will be cut out anyway! It's often the warm-up to the "real" story.)

- **If all else fails…just write.** Sometimes it helps just to write anything related to the story. Students can write a descriptive paragraph about the main character or the setting or a section of dialogue between two characters. This getting-the-juices-flowing writing can help unplug the dam which is keeping the story locked up.

Mini-lesson _____

Your Title Here

Goal

Help students brainstorm an original, creative title.

Teacher Preparation

None.

Instructional Task

Students who haven't already decided on a title should list words, ideas, or images which are central to their stories and then experiment with different combinations of adjectives, nouns, and verbs. Encourage them to include words which will hook a reader. For example, "The Diary," "Michael's Soccer Game," or "Snow Day" are not very intriguing titles. "The Tattered Diary," "Michael's Final Soccer Game," and "The Unwanted Snow Day" raise questions in the reader's mind. Remind students to capitalize the first, last, and all other important words.

Mini-lesson _____

"The End"

Goal

Help students brainstorm a realistic and satisfactory ending to their stories.

Teacher Preparation

Chapter_5:
The End

- Make a transparency and copies of **"The End"** (p. 118).
- Write the following quote by Damon Knight, the late science fiction writer on the board:

> "Think of an ending. The first ending you think of is the one everyone expects. So discard it. Think of a second ending. Discard that one, too. Think of a third ending. That's the one to use."

Instructional Tasks

Use the following questions to stimulate thought:

- What did the character accomplish or fail to accomplish?
- What did meeting his goal mean to the character?
- What decision does the character make which provides a satisfactory conclusion to his problem?
- How does this decision reflect his weaknesses and strengths?

Discuss "million dollar" endings. Often beginning writers want to resolve their characters' problems in a magical way: a character will wake up, find out that he has won the lottery, get on TV, move into a mansion, and become the most popular kid in school. Unfortunately, these Cinderella-type endings are not only rare in reality, but also make lousy endings for stories. Just like the "Wake up and find out it's all a dream" ending, or the "Talent scout/rich uncle/long-lost relative rescues the athlete/artist/actor from a life of poverty/misery/disease" story, magical resolutions cheat the reader out of getting inside a *real* character that learns and grows as he struggles with *real* problems.

Emphasize creating *simple* problems that the character can resolve without divine, magical, or adult intervention. If Carolyn's main problem was that her dog Jazz was lost, the way that she went about finding him (and the obstacles she met in the process) showed her character as well as built tension in the story.

A writer shouldn't let Carolyn's mother, father, big brother, or the local friendly policeman find Jazz for her!

Remind students that not all endings are happy—characters can learn to live with unmet goals. The important thing is that the presented problem is resolved and there is closure to the story.

Put **"The End"** on the overhead and discuss the different types of endings which students can use.

"The End"

The Surprise Ending. Although you have planted "clues" along the way, this ending is unexpected. This believable ending leaves the reader feeling satisfied that all parts of the story make sense.

The Character Has Changed Ending. If your character is going to change, show him wrestling with these issues throughout the story.

The Beginning Ending. Like bookends, if you take dialogue, thoughts, or events from the beginning and use them again at the end, it ties the story together. For example, the character can be doing the same thing he was doing at the beginning, but the people or situation have changed.

The Dialogue Ending. Have a character say something memorable at the end. This may or may not refer to the title.

The Decision Ending. Leave the reader with an important decision which your character makes that will influence the rest of her life. For example:

> "Luella knew that her brother was right. She probably would be flogged again, but inside she knew that one day, her chains would be history."

The Play with Words Ending. Take a word or idea from the story and turn it on its head by using it in a different way. For example, the word box can mean several things. An ending like, "Margaret knew that she would never be boxed in again" might work in a story which had used the word box in a different context.

"The End" Ending. End the story when the action in the story is complete. For example:

> "When Eduardo's train pulled into the station, he breathed a sigh of relief. He was home."

Adapted from materials by Robert Elmer. Used with permission.

Editing and Revising

This block of lessons provides guidelines for the critiquing and revising process which should flow between the writer, peer editor, and teacher. Hopefully, ever since the **Red Pencil** mini-lesson (p. 31), your students have experienced the rewards of editing and revising their work. If that is true, then this round of editing will be a natural outgrowth of the entire course of writing a short story.

In this phase of the story-writing process, students will learn how to recycle some of their treasures, take criticism without being defensive, benefit from their mistakes, and stick with it to "The End."

Likewise, as editors, student will learn how to analyze their peers' work and give thoughtful, positive feedback. As they do this, their own critical thinking skills develop. The more *show, don't tell* activities that the students have been exposed to during this unit, the better prepared they will be to spot errors and offer constructive criticism. Just like writing, critiquing is also learned gradually and builds on previous experience. Your students' critiques will become more thoughtful as they practice critiquing their peers.

In theory, the critiquing process looks like this:

1. A student uses **FMEs—Frequently Made Errors** and makes appropriate changes. He evaluates his own story by reviewing his plot sentence and **Build-a-Plot**. (See the **Self Critique** mini-lesson on p. 123.)

2. A peer editor thoughtfully takes time to critique the story and make suggestions using either the generic **Peer Checklist** (p. 129) or a genre peer checklist. The author chooses which suggestions to incorporate into his story. (See the **Peer Editing** mini-lesson on p. 125.)

3. The writer turns in a final rough draft to the teacher, who makes one last round of suggestions using **Strategies for Revision** (p. 130). Use this reproducible to individualize your feedback to each student. After you read a student's story, consider which areas are the most important for your student to focus on. You might decide that a beginning writer needs to think primarily about her story's organization so your comments might point out her need to have a logical progression of events, how to include transitions, and suggestions for paragraph breaks. A more advanced writer might be able to think about how the story doesn't show why his character acts the way he does or suggestions about including dialogue. Return a copy of **Strategies for Revision** to each student along with your comments on their rough draft.

4. The writer chooses which suggestions to incorporate into his revised, polished story.

Your classroom reality won't always match that picture. A particular student will want a specific friend to read his story first; peers won't want to hurt each other's feelings or won't know how to provide constructive feedback; your carefully assigned partners won't quite work out because one student is sick, another left his story at home, and a third hasn't written her ending yet. Flexibility is key. The important thing is that within your time constraints, each writer receives as much constructive feedback as possible from both his peers and from you.

Conferencing

How many times should you read your students' work? That is a difficult call. Some students will want your opinion on every revision they make. But time constraints and a stack of stories on your desk make that as impossible as getting progress reports done on the same night that your in-laws drop by for dinner. Accepting the story only when the writer has done her best encourages excellence as well as underscores the writer's ownership. It also avoids burning you out as the editor-with-all-of-the-answers.

Read each story at least once. But if you find yourself driving home from school worrying about how a student's character is going to resolve his problem, you've probably gone too far. Remember, it is the student's story, not yours. When Maity Schrecengost (educator and author of *Writing Whizardry*) is asked to comment on a story, she throws the question back in the writer's lap with, "What do YOU think?" It's a great place to start.

Your ten- to fifteen-minute conference with each student should be as private as possible. Establish boundary lines around your desk. Students should know that when an author is sitting in the critique chair next to you, the two of you are not to be disturbed. Instructing students to respect this time and space will encourage the entire class to prize this one-on-one time with you. Keep your eyes on the clock. Students might not want to leave once they have gained that seat.

Don't just hand your students a marked-up copy of their stories. Encourage them to take notes and ask questions. Don't just tell them how to fix a problem, show them why they might want to consider changing a scene or dialogue.

Overuse of Description

Sometimes in the excitement of using new skills, students can misuse or overuse them. You may receive descriptive paragraphs like this: "The wind blew peacefully as a lioness chasing a zebra. Leaves of all different colors were scattered along the ground like broken plastic cups that a giant crashed to the ground. Bare branches poked out of the tree like huge monsters fingers. The day smelled as gorgeous as a bed of roses."

Not only do some of the images conflict—*a lioness chasing a zebra* isn't peaceful, a *gorgeous day* doesn't fit the mood of *monsters fingers,* and fallen *leaves* don't look like *broken plastic cups*—but this paragraph is burdened with so much description that the reader doesn't know what to think!

Unfortunately, these descriptive passages are often the ones the writer *loves* and can't imagine cutting. Although these "word treasures" may contain wonderful images, similes, and adjectives, they are often too long and don't move the story along.

Encourage students to ask themselves, "If this paragraph or sentence were cut or shortened, would my story still make sense?" (This is also a great entry for helping students who are running over the word limit.) And instead of trashing their "word treasures," encourage students to save them in a separate folder. These small writing pieces can be the genesis of a poem or another story.

Underuse of Description

Frequently students begin a story with strong, *showing* descriptions. Although the first paragraphs are interesting and descriptive, by the middle of the second page, the author tires and returns to a litany of events. Identifying when the author has started to *tell* the story, rather than *show* it, can be extremely helpful to a writer.

Misuse of Dialogue

In an attempt to incorporate conversations into their stories, students may use dialogue for unimportant exchanges between characters. Remind students to use dialogue to give the reader more information about the character or important events in the story.

Paragraph Doesn't Make Sense or Information Is Missing

When you read a paragraph or passage that doesn't make sense, prompt the writer to explain what she was trying to say. Verbalizing frequently helps the writer clarify her language. Sometimes it helps the writer realize that she hasn't quite figured it out herself! If something's not clear to the writer, it won't be clear to the reader.

Grading

Following the conferences, students will revise their stories for the last time. Use **Guidelines for Grading Stories** (p. 132) to determine an appropriate grade. Once again, the goals you have chosen for your students will determine which components of the story you'll evaluate. It is also helpful to provide a written critique indicating what the student has done well, the reasons he lost points, and areas he should work on in the future.

Mini-lesson

Self-Critique

Goal

Students will carefully evaluate their own story and make necessary changes.

Teacher Preparation

• Write a quote from **Advice from the Experts** (in the Chapter_1 folder on the Resource CD) on the board.

• Make a transparency and copies of **FMEs—Frequently Made Errors** (p. 124).

Chapter_6: FME

Instructional Tasks

Briefly review **The Writing-Revising Cycle** (p. 34) and remind students that revision is an essential part of the writing process. Refer back to previous in-class examples.

Put **FMEs—Frequently Made Errors** on the overhead and review.

If possible, students should (quietly!) read their stories out loud to themselves *exactly* as it is written. (Suggest that students go into the hall or move their desks apart so that their neighbor's voice doesn't bother them.) This allows the students to find mistakes that they have missed on the screen or on paper. Armed with their red pencils or highlighters, students should mark those sentences and paragraphs that should be eliminated or revised; circle any spelling, grammar, or punctuation errors; and insert missing words.

Direct students to re-read their plot sentences and **Build-a-Plots** and consider whether they have written the stories they intended to write or if their stories have gone off track. At this point, students may recognize that they need to add or delete parts of their stories.

Tip: *"The End" is near—are your students and volunteers ready to wrap up this unit?*

Looking Ahead

Students should bring in a revised, clean copy of their stories to the next class period.

FMEs—Frequently Made Errors

Directions

Check each item only *after* you have answered each question.

Check Your Content

☐ Are there "word treasures" that are too long or really aren't necessary for the story?

☐ Do all the sentences or paragraphs make sense?

☐ Is the story told in narrative rather than shown through the character's feelings, actions, speech, and thoughts? (Is the character shown **FAST**?)

☐ Have you begun close to the problem or did you start off with long paragraphs of background or description?

☐ Have all of the conflicts been resolved by the main character?

Proofread for

☐ Spelling errors. (Particularly ones which spell check doesn't pick up. Example: homonyms such as *too, to,* and *two*)

☐ Grammar errors. (Example: Are there misplaced modifiers?)

☐ Punctuation errors. (Example: Are quotes used appropriately for dialogue? Are apostrophes used correctly?)

☐ Capitalization errors. (Example: Are all proper names capitalized, including "Mom" and "Dad" when used to address the individual?)

☐ Tense errors. Have you begun the story in the present and switched to the past?

☐ Formatting errors. Are paragraphs indented? Text double spaced? Any extra lines between paragraphs?

Mini-lesson

Peer Editing

Goal

Students will be prepared to critique their peer's story.

Teacher Preparation

- Write a quote from **Advice from the Experts** (in the Chapter_1 folder on the Resource CD) on the board.
- Make copies and an overhead of **Wanted: A Good Editor** (p. 127).
- Make copies of **Peer Critiquing Rules** (p. 128).
- Make copies of **Peer Checklist** (p. 129) or the appropriate genre-specific peer checklist from the Resource CD.

Chapter_6:
Editing Guidelines
Critiquing Rules
Peer Checklist

Instructional Tasks

Review or hand out **Peer Critiquing Rules** and **Wanted: A Good Editor**. Remind editors *not* try to re-write the story they are reading. This is their peer's story, not theirs.

Emphasize that students should first consider the *content* of the entire story before making line edits. There is little point in correcting mechanical errors such as capitalization, punctuation, and spelling until the author is near a final draft, since so many changes are made up until that point.

Make sure that the same student doesn't get "volunteered" into being the peer editor all the time. Some students are naturally good editors and can end up spending more time on their peers' stories than on their own.

Assign peer editors. Students swap stories and, using a red pencil or marker, carefully read and comment on their partner's story. Each editor fills out a **Peer Checklist** for each story.

Noise control can be an issue during this lesson. Be as creative as possible in finding space for your students to work. Try using an empty classroom, locker room, hallway, or book corner to separate groups from one another. Circulate among the groups to answer questions and make sure that students stay on task.

Modifications

In order to focus on content first, you can divide the process into two steps. First, students read each other's story and evaluate the content. Second, students read the story and look for mechanical errors.

You can also use small groups for this process. In a revision group of three or four, students take turns reading their stories out loud and receive feedback about the content. Then the groups break down into partners and look at each other's grammar, spelling, punctuation, etc.

If the peer checklist appears overwhelming to your students, select which criteria you want your students to focus on.

Working in a group, students are each assigned one aspect on which to focus their critique. For example, after reading the story and correcting verb tenses, a student passes the story to another peer editor who checks that the character is clearly shown.

Looking Ahead

Students review the critique which they have received, decide which suggestions they want to include, and make appropriate revisions. They should clip together their **Build-a-Plot**, plot sentence, and completed rough draft and bring them in the following day.

Wanted: A Good Editor

Story editor needed. Required skills include ability to think critically, to be patient, and to encourage. Good humor helps. Payment is given in like services received.

Job description:

1. Read (or listen to) the entire story before commenting.
2. Review the author's plot sentence and **Build-a-Plot**. Ask yourself:
   - Is the character's problem clear?
   - Can you see and hear the character? Can you tell how he is feeling?
   - Can you picture this setting in your mind?
   - Are the more major events well defined?
   - What is the climax?
   - Is the problem resolved by the main character?
3. Honestly answer the following questions:
   - Did this story capture your interest from the beginning?
   - Did this story open with action, description, or background?
   - Did your mind wander while reading it?
   - Did this story make sense or were there parts that were confusing?
   - Did the similes, metaphors, and other descriptive language used fit the mood and setting of the story?

Peer Critiquing Rules

1. **Take your job seriously**. Providing helpful suggestions can be as difficult as writing.

2. **Be positive and constructive**. Sandwich your criticism between layers of positive comments about the story.

3. **Be specific**. "This is a really bad story" isn't helpful. Neither is, "I like your story." General comments will not help the writer improve his work.

4. **Be encouraging**. Help the author remember that polishing a story will make it more interesting for others to read.

5. **Whisper**. In order for this time to be constructive, peer-editing teams need to work as quietly as possible.

6. **Don't over-critique**. No one enjoys getting their stories returned and covered in red!

7. **Be neat**. Make sure that your comments are legible.

8. **Highlight nuggets** of good writing.

9. **Look to see if the story is balanced** between the beginning, middle, and end. A general rule is to have 25% in the beginning, 25% in the ending, and 50% in the middle.

Peer Checklist

Directions

Using a scale of 1-5 (with 5 being the best), score the criteria listed below. Write additional comments on the back of this page.

- ☐ You showed the character's main problem clearly.

- ☐ You focused on a short amount of time.

- ☐ The events which the character faced in resolving his problem were clear.

- ☐ The sequence of events made sense.

- ☐ The character resolved his problem himself.

- ☐ Events and settings are *shown*, not just *told*.

- ☐ You *showed* how the character felt and thought.

- ☐ You used the same tense throughout the whole story.

- ☐ You told the story from the same perspective (i.e., first or third person).

- ☐ You used strong, active verbs.

- ☐ You used adjectives and adverbs appropriately.

- ☐ You used dialogue effectively.

- ☐ You don't always use "said" in dialogue. (Examples: *whined*, *shouted*, etc.)

- ☐ At least one time you used a simile, metaphor, or other creative language which enhanced the story.

- ☐ There is a good balance between the beginning, middle, and end.

- ☐ The title fits and is intriguing.

- ☐ You used complete sentences with correct spelling, grammar, capitalization, and punctuation.

Strategies for Revision

Overall Content

- ☐ Improve the story by making it more believable.
- ☐ Improve the story by making sure that everything makes sense. Look at the paragraphs and sentences I have underlined, which are not clear.
- ☐ Maintain the same point of view throughout the entire story. Note examples I have circled.
- ☐ Maintain the same tense throughout the entire story. Note examples I have circled.
- ☐ Improve the story by including more genre-specific details.

Beginning, Middle, and End

- ☐ Improve the beginning by adding information which the reader needs to understand the total story.
- ☐ Improve the beginning by deleting overly-descriptive paragraphs. Select key details and good sentences to weave into the main body of the story.
- ☐ Improve the middle by showing a clear progression of events.
- ☐ Include transitions that contribute to the flow of the story.
- ☐ Improve the end by showing the character resolving the problem and giving the story a sense of overall completeness.
- ☐ Make sure every event in the writing helps to tell the story. Take out "bunny trails" which take the reader away from the main story.

Show, Don't Tell

- [ ] Add details which show what your character looks like and how he reacts to situations.
- [ ] Add details which explain the character's motivation for reaching his goal.
- [ ] Add details by showing what your character feels or thinks.
- [ ] Add details by showing the scene. (Remember <u>all</u> the senses.)
- [ ] Add details by showing an important event.
- [ ] Add details by including dialogue.
- [ ] Create vivid visual images by using metaphors and similes.

Mechanics

- [ ] Improve sentences by combining short, choppy sentences into longer, smoother sentences.
- [ ] Use strong, active verbs—eliminate passive "ing" verbs. Say, "Lydia pet the poodle" rather than, "The poodle was petted by Lydia."
- [ ] Shorten paragraphs. Change paragraphs with each new speaker and when the subject changes.
- [ ] Make your antecedents clear. Note underlined examples.
- [ ] Correct your punctuation and capitalization.

Guidelines for Grading Stories

Overall Structure (UP TO 30 POINTS)

Points are awarded if the story

- Is original and creative
- Has a believable plot
- Has an interesting opening
- Flows well, has good transitions
- Shows genre (if appropriate)

Body (UP TO 30 POINTS)

Points are awarded if the story

- Shows characters who are believable and consistent
- Shows setting which fits the story's mood
- Shows character's problem and events he goes through to resolve the problem
- Has appropriate use of dialogue

Conclusion (UP TO 15 POINTS)

Points are awarded if the character's problem is resolved appropriately.

Grammar and Mechanics (UP TO 25 POINTS)

Points are taken away if the story

- Has grammatical errors, including spelling, punctuation, and capitalization
- Shows poor sentence structure and syntax
- Is not neat and easy to read

Mini-lesson _____

After "The End"

Congratulations! You have coached your students through the process of writing a short story. Each student has stretched his imagination, used a toolbox full of writing skills, and learned to critically analyze a peer's written work. That is a milestone for many middle-school students. If possible, take time to celebrate this achievement.

There are many different ways you can mark the end of this unit.

Party Time

It only takes soda, chips, or brownies for middle-school students to think *party*. But you can also tie the party food into your students' genres and suggest they bring in things like fantasy chip and dip (onion dip dyed blue), ginger snaps from the Civil War period, or hockey-puck cupcakes.

For a fun activity at your party, hold a "Write Off." Choose one of the criteria listed below:

1. Best paragraph that shows a character
2. Best paragraph that shows a setting
3. Best section of dialogue
4. Best paragraph that shows the character's problem
5. Best paragraph which makes the reader want to find out what happens next

Taking turns, students stand up and read the appropriate section of their stories. Any student who thinks his selection is better can stand up and challenge the previous writer. You, or the class, decide which author remains in the contest until the end. Limit the number of challenges per student if you have a large class.

You could also invite students to come to class dressed as their main character. They push their desks to the walls, kick off their shoes, sit in small groups on the floor, and listen to each other's stories. Pass the popcorn and enjoy!

Publication

As much as a painter wants to display his finished artwork in a gallery, every writer wants a reader. There are several ways in which your students can share their stories with an audience.

With the help of a parent volunteer, you could print an anthology of the students' stories that each student gets to keep. Searching the Internet under "bookbinding lesson plans" will provide ideas on how to bind the book. Or even simpler, autographed copies of each story can go into a binder which you keep and use as an example next year. Either of these types of anthologies may include illustrations, special fonts, or calligraphy.

Students can display completed stories and/or anthologies at a PTA meeting, open house, book fair, or media center. Selected stories can be posted on the school's website. Students can submit their stories to the school literary magazine for consideration. Stories could also be serialized and published in the school newspaper.

Contests

Judging forms and instructions for holding a classroom, grade-level, or school-wide writing contest sponsored by your Friends of the Library Association or PTA can be found in the Chapter_6 folder on the Resource CD in the **Contests and Judging** subfolder. The promise of prizes (modest gift certificates to local stores) really motivates middle-school students. Publishing the winning stories in a small booklet also adds to the prestige of winning the contest.

In addition, there are many writing contests and opportunities for young writers to get published, both in print and online. Check the **Getting Published** file under the Chapter_6 folder on the Resource CD. It lists websites with information about different contests. Feel free to add to it and save it to your computer. Remember to check for outdated links before printing copies for your students. Search the Internet using "writing contests + middle schools" or "teens write + stories" to find additional sites.

Emphasize that students must carefully follow contest guidelines. You can require your students to enter at least one writing contest during the school year or offer extra credit for those who do. Make sure that contest winners are acknowledged in your school paper or website. Students (and their parents) love to see their names in print.

Author Visit

You can find a local author by asking your local librarian or by going to http://www.scbwi.org/regions.htm and clicking on your region.

If possible, talk with the visiting author before he arrives to get an idea of how much time he will have and what he plans on discussing. Prepare your students for the visit. Consider having your students read pre-selected sections from their stories. Finish with the author reading from one of his books. A book signing and refreshments could follow.

Resources

Atwell, Nancie. *In the Middle*. Portsmouth: Heinemann, 1998.

Bell, Theodore Scott. "Fiction: Stretching the Tension." *Writer's Digest*, Aug. 2003.

Brooks, Terry. *The Writer's Complete Fantasy Reference*. Cincinnati: Writer's Digest Books, 1998.

Card, Orson Scott. *How to Write Science Fiction and Fantasy*. Cincinnati: Writer's Digest Books, 1990.

Carver, Jeffrey. "Writing Science Fiction and Fantasy" in *Studyworks! Science Deluxe* (versions 4–5). Cambridge, Mass: MathSoft, 2000. CD-ROM.

Hayden, G. Miki. *Writing the Mystery: A Start to Finish Guide for Both Novice and Professional*. Philadelphia: Intrigue Press, 2001.

Henderon, Kathy. *The Young Writer's Guide to Getting Published*, Cincinnati: Writer's Digest Books, 2001.

Koehler-Pentacoff, Liz. "Ending Your Middle Grade Novel." *ByLine*, Oct. 2004.

Lukeman, Noah. "The Heights." *Writer's Digest*, Nov. 2003.

Martin, Rhona. *Writing Historical Fiction*. New York: St. Martin's Press, 1988.

Schrecengost, Maity. *Writing Whizardry*. Gainesville, FL: Maupin House Publishing, 2001.

Van Alsburg, Chris. *Mysteries of Harris*. New York: Houghton Mifflin, 1984.

Resource CD Contents

Chapter_1

Advice from the Experts
Blank Libs
Defining Historical Fiction
Defining Mystery
Defining SciFi Fantasy
Defining Sports
Dont Tell Me about Rabbits
Genre Story Prompts
Helpful Websites for Research
How to Teach—Red Pencil
Parent-Teacher Letter
Recommended Reading Lists
Ten Hints
Tips 4 U
Whose Point Is It Anyway
Writing-Revising Cycle

Chapter_2

Bank—Fantasy Antagonist
Bank—Historical Character
Bank—Mystery Character
Bank—SciFi Character
Bank—Sports Character
Character Info Bank
Create Imaginary Characters
Describe Your Character
Dialogue or Not
Dialogue Tips
Getting to Know You
Give Em a Fight
How Does this Sound
How to Teach—Antagonist
How to Teach—Character
How to Teach—Detective
How to Teach—Historical Character
How to Teach—SciFi Character
How to Teach—Sports Character
Key Character Details—Genres
Name Him What
Said This Better
Show Dont Tell—Character
Show Dont Tell—Fantasy
Show Dont Tell—History
Show Dont Tell—Sports
Who Is This Character

Chapter_3

Fantasy Setting Bank
How Moody Is Your Setting
How to Teach—Fantasy Setting

How to Teach—Mystery Setting
How to Teach—Sports Setting
How to Teach—Setting
Launch Your Story
Mystery Setting Bank
Openings That Grab
Setting Information Bank
Setting Worksheet
Sports Setting Bank
Student Historical Settings
Student Mysterious Settings
Student Samples Setting
Student Sports Settings
What Could Happen Here

Chapter_4

Bear Attack
Build-a-Plot—Blank
Build-a-Plot—Historical
Build-a-Plot—Mystery
Build-a-Plot—SciFi
Build-a-Plot—Sports
Plan-a-Problem
Plot Props
Problems Characters Can Handle
Real Life Problems
Up the Ante

Chapter_5

Not a Novel
The End
Useful Transitions

Chapter_6

Checklist—History
Checklist—Mystery
Checklist—SciFi_Fantasy
Checklist—Sports
Critiquing Rules
Editing Guidelines
FME
Getting Published
Grading Guidelines
Peer Checklist
Strategies for Revision
Contests and Judging
    Contest Info
      Judging Guidelines
      Judging Form